PERSPECTIVE

Edited by
Kenneth Gillam

Associate Editors

Kathryn Bennett

Megan Hoelting

Tristin Hooker

Cynthia Johnson

Aubrey Larimore

Kandice McKee

Heather Messick

Natalie Monzyk

Andrew Myers

Eden Olena

Shiloh Peters

Erik Renth

Linda Tinson

Wendy Wallace

Satarah Wheeler

Bambi Whitaker

FOUNTAINHEAD PRESS

Our green initiatives include:

Electronic Products
We deliver products in non-paper form whenever possible. This includes pdf downloadables, flash drives, & CDs.

Electronic Samples
We use Xample, a new electronic sampling system. Instructor samples are sent via a personalized web page that links to pdf downloads.

FSC Certified Printers
All of our printers are certified by the Forest Service Council which promotes environmentally and socially responsible management of the world's forests. This program allows consumer groups, individual consumers, and businesses to work together hand-in-hand to promote responsible use of the world's forests as a renewable and sustainable resource.

Recycled Paper
Most of our products are printed on a minimum of 30% post-consumer waste recycled paper.

Support of Green Causes
When we do print, we donate a portion of our revenue to green causes. Listed below are a few of the organizations that have received donations from Fountainhead Press. We welcome your feedback and suggestions for contributions, as we are always searching for worthy initiatives.
Rainforest 2 Reef
Environmental Working Group

Design by Susan Moore

Books may be purchased for educational purposes.

For information, please call or write:

1-800-586-0330

Fountainhead Press
Southlake, TX 76092

Web Site: www.fountainheadpress.com
E-mail: customerservice@fountainheadpress.com

First Edition

ISBN: 978-1-59871-715-0

Printed in the United States of America

TABLE OF CONTENTS

INTRODUCTION

By Erik Renth

"...I started the class by picking up a chair and placing it in front of me. What do you see? I asked the class. A chair. Then I placed the chair upside down. Not what do you see? Still a chair. Then I straightened the chair and asked a few students to stand in different places around the room, and asked both those standing and those sitting to describe the same chair. You see this is a chair, but when you come to describe it, you do so from where you are positioned, and from your own perspective, and so you cannot say there is only one way of seeing a chair, can you? No, obviously not. If you cannot say this about so simple an object as a chair, how can you possibly pass absolute judgment on any given individual?"

Reading Lolita *in Tehran: A Memoir in Stories*
—Azar Nafisi

You have your own perspective. Your experiences, your religion, your thoughts, your political affiliations, and so many other facets of you— they all make up a unique perspective that cannot be replicated, at least not in whole. No one else can see the chair from the exact point that you are sitting; no one else can experience that vision in quite the same way. Your perspective is unique, but it isn't the only perspective that exists—it isn't the only valid perspective. There will always be others sitting at a different point in the room, seeing from a different place. Such is the nature of life, though. There will always be others seeing life unfold from a different locale, a different angle, a different perspective.

As every individual approaches the same issue, he or she brings all of those experiences and thoughts as well. Those things that we bring to our perspective are our understanding and make up our culture. We find commonality through our cultural identities; we are able to identify with similar viewpoints, and those bind us to other people who share our cultural identities. We have the propensity to share many things and many views through our culture, and that helps to shape a collective viewpoint.

Think of the chair at the front of the classroom once more. You're the only person who can see the chair from that very angle, but think of the commonality you all see in the chair. It is made of wood. It has a red seat, a crooked leg. You all see this, and this is your common experience. It binds you all, in a way. That isn't to say that culture is universal, though. Wonder what it would be like to experience it from another perspective. Would it be different? You could go stand in the same spot as one of your peers and try to see what they see. But could you experience that viewpoint in the exact same way? It would be difficult to notice the sloped back, the red seat, or the type of wood in quite the same way. What you call a maroon, another might call crimson. But more than that; how your culture uses chairs, if it has chairs at all, will inform your experiences and memories, which go on to shade all meanings. Though you're standing in the same place, the experiences vary.

In the same way, personal cultures vary. All of the cultures and experiences that make up each individual in the room means that each will experience it in in a novel way. It is by embracing and empathizing with those differences that we can learn to reach a level of understanding with others. No one person is more right about how the chair looks, though. It's all about where each person in the room is coming from. And, just as important as the way see the chair is that we think of how everyone else in the room can see the chair—those perspectives are all integral to the collective experience. In much the same way, it is important to be sensitive to the cultures we encounter in an increasingly global society. In *Education for the Intercultural Experience,* Milton J. Benett presents a model of intercultural sensitivity, which is defined as seeing one's own culture as central to reality. As an individual moves from Ethnocentric to Ethnorelative stages, he or she becomes more able to relate within diverse cultural spheres and usurps the tendency to view his or her own cultural identity as a paragon. The stages are shown below.

ETHNOCENTRIC STAGES

Denial: This is the first of the stages, and people in this stage are the most ethnocentric. People in in the denial stage often fail to see differences between cultures, ignore those differences, or intentionally isolate themselves from such differences to protect their own worldview. Those in denial are genuinely disinterested in understanding other cultures.

Defense: The stage of defense is the first stage in which cultural differences are recognized. However, a person in the defense stage is denigrating to other cultures and openly vocal about the superiority of his or her own culture. While this may not seem like a less ethnocentric viewpoint, the willingness of those people in the defense stage to recognize cultural differences is an important, albeit small, step forward.

Minimalization: In this last stage of ethnocentrism, there is a shift toward understanding the global population as a whole. While the denigration of other cultures has weaned in a person in the minimalization stage, differences between the cultures are, in this stage, minimalized or romanticized. Thus, a person in this stage is susceptible to stereotyping.

ETHNORELATIVE STAGES

Acceptance: Acceptance is the first stage in which a person not only recognizes that there are multiple, complex worldviews but also accepts those as valid. While a person in this stage may still think his or her culture is the most valid, he or she has the ability to recognize that his or her thoughts are born out of a particular cultural experience.

Adaptation: In the adaptation stage, people become more empathetic to the cultures of others, and they have developed the interpersonal communication skills to effectively communicate crossculturally. This is the first stage in which a person may see the world through several integrated worldviews and has the insight to behave appropriately across a broad range of cultural situations.

Integration: The final stage of the continuum, integration, sees the breakdown of traditional cultural roles. A person in this stage of the continuum may be able to see past traditional cultural barriers to evaluate a situation. The "I" becomes more than merely a viewpoint from any particular culture; rather, it is a constantly changing and evolving perspective.

No two people will ever see the world in exactly the same way. However, it is our duty to continue in the pursuit of understanding the vision of others in an attempt to find a more global perspective. This book was assembled with that end in mind. The editors chose the specific articles in the book to illustrate the various aspects of culture. From the pageantry of Bollywood to the advancement of robotics for use by the aging population and Walt Whitman and the Civil War, these articles help *Perspective* to illuminate the diversity of global culture, to move the reader toward ethnorelativity and the integration of cultures into his or her own viewpoints. It is our hope that these articles will help you to think of other perspectives—ones you may not have been able to experience before—as you move through your everyday life and to see the world as something that is more than just what you can see from where you stand.

Max Fisher is a current blogger for the Washington Post, *focusing on foreign affairs and international policies. He is is a former author and editor at* The Atlantic.

WELCOME TO AMERICA, PLEASE BE ON TIME

BY MAX FISHER

WHAT GUIDE BOOKS TELL FOREIGN VISITORS TO THE U.S.

Such tips as "don't hand out cash to dinner guests" reveal what foreign tourists find surprising about coming to America.

The United States is the second greatest tourist draw in the world, with 60-million-plus visitors in 2010 alone (France, number one, attracted almost 80 million). Flipping through a few of the many English-language tourist guides provides a fascinating, if non-scientific and narrow, window into how people from the outside world perceive America, Americans, and the surprises and pitfalls of spending time here.

Of the many pieces of advice proffered, four of the most common are eat with your fingers (sometimes), arrive on time (always), don't drink and drive (they take it seriously here!), and be careful about talking politics (unless you've got some time to spare). But they say more than that.

One of the first things you notice in picking up *Lonely Planet USA* or *Rough Guides: The USA* or reading WikiTravel's United States of America page, as I did (traditional guides such as *Fodor's* or *Frommer's* are more circumspect and not nearly as interesting), is the surprising frankness in discussing the warts of American history and society. The

9

destruction of native communities and slavery both get long sections, the latter usually including some comments on still-present racial sensitivities.

"Gifts of cash, prepared ready-to-serve foods, or very personal items (e.g. toiletries) are not appropriate."

Politics get heavy treatment in the books, as do the subtleties of discussing them, maybe more so than in any other guidebook I've read (what can I say, it's an addiction). *Lonely Planet* urges caution when discussing immigration. "This is the issue that makes Americans edgy, especially when it gets politicized," they write, subtly suggesting that some Americans might approach the issue differently than others. "Age has a lot to do with Americans' multicultural tolerance."

Rough Guide doesn't shy away from the fact that many non-Americans are less-than-crazy about U.S. politics and foreign policy and encouragingly notes that many Americans are just as "infuriated" about it as visitors might be. Still, it warns that the political culture saturates everything, and that "The combination of shoot-from-the-hip mentality with laissez-faire capitalism and religious fervor can make the U.S. maddening at times, even to its own residents." They go on:

> Vigour and passion are animating forces in politics and culture here. While this tendency has deep roots in the country's religious heritage (modern evangelism was perfected here), it affects everything from the firm opinions people hold over even trivial matters, to the public stand they make over God, government, guns, and other incendiary topics.

Lonely Planet even offers a helpful tip for navigating the polarized politics, in which political truth can be hard to come by, particularly "during election cycles." They recommend fact.check.org: "It's a great resource for parsing truth from political bombast." Sometimes, the books seem to assume that foreign visitors might have a tough time navigating the redder parts of America. "Texas is the country's capital for oil-drilling, BBQ-eating and right-wing politicking, with huge expanses of land and equally domineering attitudes," says *Rough*

Guide. Lonely Planet says that solo women travelers in "rural" areas can sometimes attract raised eyebrows.

But maybe the topic that gets the most attention in these books is food, which they praise for its quality and variety (and portion size) in a tone of near-disbelief. As in any culture, the niceties of dining—especially at someone's home—can get complicated. Here, from Wikitravel, is some sage advice on a ritual that even I did not realize was so complicated until I read this passage:

> When invited to a meal in a private home, it is considered polite for a guest to ask if they can bring anything for the meal, such as a dessert, a side dish, or for an outdoor barbecue, something useful like ice or plastic cups, plates. The host will usually refuse except among very close friends, but it is nonetheless considered good manners to bring along a small gift for the host. A bottle of wine, box of candies or fresh cut flowers are most common. Gifts of cash, prepared ready-to-serve foods, or very personal items (e.g. toiletries) are not appropriate.

Wikitravel has you covered for going out to restaurants: don't plop down at a stranger's table, don't slurp, and don't pick up your cell phone. There is one piece of good news: it is not considered rude to leave some food on your plate. If you've ever made the mistake of over-ordering in a culture where eating less than everything can be a profound insult, you know how much of a relief this American standard can be:

> It is usually inappropriate to join a table already occupied by other diners, even if it has unused seats; Americans prefer this degree of privacy when they eat. Exceptions are cafeteria-style eateries with long tables, and at crowded informal eateries and cafes you may have success asking a stranger if you can share the table they're sitting at. Striking up a conversation in this situation may or may not be welcome, however.
>
> Table manners, while varying greatly, are typically European influenced. Slurping or making other noises while

> eating are considered rude, as is loud conversation (including
> phone calls). [...] Offense isn't taken if you don't finish your
> meal, and most restaurants will package the remainder to
> take with you, or provide a box for you to do this yourself
> (sometimes euphemistically called a "doggy bag," implying
> that the leftovers are for your pet). If you want to do this,
> ask the server to get the remainder "to go"; this term will
> be almost universally understood and will not cause any
> embarrassment. Some restaurants offer an "all-you-can-
> eat" buffet or other service; taking home portions from such
> a meal is either not allowed or carries an additional fee.

You might say that global food cultures tend to fall into one of two
categories: utensil cultures and finger cultures. The U.S., somewhat
unusually, has both: the appropriate delivery method can vary between
cuisines, and even between dishes, and it's far from obvious which is
which. Baked chicken is a fork food, but fried chicken a finger food,
depending on how it's fried. If you get fried pieces of potato, it's a
finger food, unless the potato retains some circular shape, in which case
use your fork. And so on. Confused yet?

The books emphasize that the U.S. is safe, with one big exception
they all note: "inner cities," which are described with a terror that can
feel a little outdated. "When driving, under no circumstances should
you stop in any unlit or seemingly deserted urban area," *Rough Guide*
warns, going on to describe dangerous scams - a strange man waving
you down for "auto trouble," another car hitting yours out of nowhere
so that you'll get out - in a way that makes them sound commonplace.

Gay and lesbian travelers are urged to stick to the big cities. "In the rural
heartland, however, life can look more like the Fifties - homosexuals
are still oppressed and commonly reviled. Gay travelers need to watch
their step to avoid hassles and possible aggression," according to *Lonely
Planet*.

Despite the divides, there is one thing that Americans agree on,
according to the guides: punctuality is a big deal. *Lonely Planet*, in
the same paragraph, notes that "Americans are notoriously informal
in their dining manners" but that "it's polite to be prompt . . . arrive

within 15 minutes of the designated time." They repeat, later, "Do be on time. Many folks in the U.S. consider it rude to be kept waiting." *Rough Guide* hammers home, in asides in many sections, that things happen on time here, and lateness doesn't get forgiven easily.

Another common tip has to do with personal space: Americans like it *a lot.* "Don't be overly physical if you meet someone," says *Lonely Planet. Rough Guide* suggests keeping arms-length distance except in the most crowded urban circumstances. Books gently deter cheek-kissing - especially outside of coastal cities - and, when it comes to the intricacies of when to hug or not hug, suggest simply following the Americans' lead.

For travel, there are long sections on visas and how to navigate airport security, along with warnings that Amtrak service can be, as the *Rough Guide* puts it, "skeletal." WikiTravel features a yellow-highlighted section warning against overstaying your visa - the country takes it quite seriously. There are three paragraphs reiterating the importance of carrying travel documents on your person when near the border.

In many ways, the tour books say as much about the world as they do about the U.S., by highlighting the ways in which American practices and standards deviate. Anyone who's traveled widely, particularly in the developing world, will understand why these books are so emphatic about, for example, punctuality, personal space, and the unreliability of our trains.

Still, these are guides for people who want to spend their time and money seeing America, and this excitement shines through even the sourest sections.

"Many of the stereotypes do hold true - this is a place where you'll find real life cowboys, gangsters, and other Hollywood standbys," *Rough Guide* says. "The palpable sense of newness here creates an odd sort of **optimism**, where anything seems possible and fortune can strike at any moment."

Update, June 3: A number of commenters ask about tipping. As I note in the comments, the books tend to include long sections on the nuances of American tipping. They also strongly encourage visitors to adhere to the unusually high tipping rates, explaining both that service jobs tend to pay very poorly and that the tipping system is partially responsible for the exceptional quality and consistency of service here. A commenter on Reddit posts this excerpt, from a guide book for the U.S. that the commenter says was translated from Japanese, explaining tipping in unusually blunt terms.

> Americans have a social institution called a "gratuity." Basically, the price on the menu at any place which serves food is not the real price. The real price is 20% higher. You have to calculate 20%, write it under the subtotal, and sum to arrive at the real price. Taxis work the same way. It is considered very rude not to pay the "gratuity."

Does Fisher's viewpoint give you a new perspective on how foreign visitors view the United States? Do you think Fisher makes any unfair observations about the United States?

Fisher discusses several issues—like physical space, tipping, and punctuality—as very important, which might imply that these are less important in other cultures. What might this article say about how people of different cultures and perspectives see similar situations?

A well known anthropologist, Dr. Horace Mitchell Miner, earned his doctorate from the University of Chicago in 1937. He served in the U.S. Army as a counterintelligence agent during World War II and became an assistant professor of sociology at the University of Michigan upon completing his service. He received many scholarly awards, including a Fulbright Research Grant, and had several publications. "Body Rituals among the Nacirema," published in American Anthropologist in June of 1956, is his most famous work. Dr. Miner died as a result of Alzheimer's disease in 1993.

BODY RITUALS AMONG THE NACIREMA

By Horace Mitchell Miner

The anthropologist has become so familiar with the diversity of ways in which different peoples behave in similar situations that he is not apt to be surprised by even the most exotic customs. In fact, if all of the logically possible combination of behavior have not been found somewhere in the world, he is apt to suspect that they must be present in some yet undescribed tribe. This point has, in fact, been expressed with respect to clan organization by Murdock (1949:71). In this light, the magical beliefs and practices of the Nacirema present such unusual aspects that it seems desirable to describe them as an example of the extremes to which human behavior can go.

Professor Linton first brought the ritual of the Nacirema to the attention of anthropologists twenty years ago (1936: 326), but the culture of this people is still very poorly understood. They are a North American group living in the territory between the Canadian Cree, the Yaqui and Tarahumare of Mexico, and the Carib and Arawak of the Antilles. Little is known of their origin, although tradition states that they came from the east. According to Nacirema mythology, their nation was originated by a culture hero, Notgnihsaw, who is otherwise known for two great feats of strength—the throwing of a piece of wampum across the river Pa-To-Mac and the chopping down of a cherry tree in which the Spirit of Truth resided.

Nacirema culture is characterized by a highly developed market economy which has evolved in a rich natural habitat. While much of the people's time is devoted to economic pursuits, a large part of the fruits of these labors and a considerable portion of the day are spent in ritual activity. The focus of this activity is the human body, the appearance and health of which loom as a dominant concern in the ethos of the people. While such a concern is certainly not unusual, its ceremonial aspects and associated philosophy are unique.

The fundamental belief underlying the whole system appears to be that the human body is ugly and that its natural tendency is to debility and disease. Incarcerated in such a body, man's only hope is to avert these characteristics through the use of the powerful influences of ritual and ceremony. Every household has one or more shrines devoted to this purpose. The more powerful individuals in the society have several shrines in their houses and, in fact, the opulence of a house is often referred to in terms of the number of such ritual centers it possesses. Most houses are of wattle and daub construction, but the shrine rooms of the more wealthy are walled with stone. Poorer families imitate the rich by applying pottery plaques to their shrine walls.

While each family has at least one such shrine, the rituals associated with it are not family ceremonies but are private and secret. The rites are normally only discussed with children, and then only during the period when they are being initiated into these mysteries. I was able, however, to establish sufficient rapport with the natives to examine these shrines and to have the rituals described to me.

The focal point of the shrine is a box or chest which is built into the wall. In this chest are kept the many charms and magical potions without which no native believes he could live. These preparations are secured from a variety of specialized practitioners. The most powerful of these are the medicine men, whose assistance must be rewarded with substantial gifts. However, the medicine men do not provide the curative potions for their clients, but decide what the ingredients should be and then write them down in an ancient and secret language. This writing is understood only by the medicine men and by the herbalists who, for another gift, provide the required charm.

The charm is not disposed of after it has served its purpose, but is placed in the charm-box of the household shrine. As these magical materials are specific for certain ills, and the real or imagined maladies of the people are many, the charm-box is usually full to overflowing. The magical packets are so numerous that people forget what their purposes were and fear to use them again. While the natives are very vague on this point, we can only assume that the idea in retaining all the old magical materials is that their presence in the charm-box, before which the body rituals are conducted, will in some way protect the worshipper.

Beneath the charm-box is a small font. Each day every member of the family, in succession, enters the shrine room, bows his head before the charm-box, mingles different sorts of holy water in the font, and proceeds with a brief rite of ablution. The holy waters are secured from the Water Temple of the community, where the priests conduct elaborate ceremonies to make the liquid ritually pure.

In the hierarchy of magical practitioners, and below the medicine men in prestige, are specialists whose designation is best translated "holy-mouth-men." The Nacirema have an almost pathological horror of and fascination with the mouth, the condition of which is believed to have a supernatural influence on all social relationships. Were it not for the rituals of the mouth, they believe that their teeth would fall out, their gums bleed, their jaws shrink, their friends desert them, and their lovers reject them. They also believe that a strong relationship exists between oral and moral characteristics. For example, there is a ritual ablution of the mouth for children, which is supposed to improve their moral fiber.

The daily body ritual performed by everyone includes a mouth-rite. Despite the fact that these people are so punctilious about care of the mouth, this rite involves a practice which strikes the uninitiated stranger as revolting. It was reported to me that the ritual consists of inserting a small bundle of hog hairs into the mouth, along with certain magical powders, and then moving the bundle in a highly formalized series of gestures.

In addition to the private mouth-rite, the people seek out a holy-mouth-man once or twice a year. These practitioners have an impressive set of paraphernalia, consisting of a variety of augers, awls, probes, and prods. The use of these objects in the exorcism of the evils of the mouth involves almost unbelievable ritual torture of the client. The holy-mouth-man opens the client's mouth and, using the above mentioned tools, enlarges any holes which decay may have created in the teeth. Magical materials are put into these holes. If there are no naturally occurring holes in the teeth, large sections of one or more teeth are gouged out so that the supernatural substance can be applied. In the client's view, the purpose of these ministrations is to arrest decay and to draw friends. The extremely sacred and traditional character of the rite is evident in the fact that the natives return to the holy-mouth-men year after year, despite the fact that their teeth continue to decay.

It is hoped that, when a thorough study of the Nacirema is made, there will be careful inquiry into the personality structure of these people. One has but to watch the gleam in the eye of a holy-mouth-man, as he jabs an awl into an exposed nerve, to suspect that a certain amount of sadism is involved. If this can be established, a very interesting pattern emerges, for most of the population shows definite masochistic tendencies. It was to these that Professor Linton referred in discussing a distinctive part of the daily body rituals which is performed only by men. This part of the rite involves scraping and lacerating the surface of the face with a sharp instrument. Special women's rites are performed only four times during each lunar month, but what they lack in frequency is made up in barbarity. As part of this ceremony, women bake their heads in small ovens for about an hour. The theoretically interesting point is that what seems to be a preponderantly masochistic people have developed sadistic specialists.

The medicine men have an imposing temple, or *lati pso*, in every community of any size. The more elaborate ceremonies required to treat very sick patients can only be performed at this temple. These ceremonies involve not only the thaumaturge, but a permanent group of vestal maidens who move sedately about the temple chambers in distinctive costume and headdress.

The *lati pso* ceremonies are so harsh that it is phenomenal that a fair proportion of the really sick natives who enter the temple ever recover. Small children whose indoctrination is still incomplete have been known to resist attempts to take them to the temple because "that is where you go to die." Despite this fact, sick adults are not only willing but eager to undergo the protracted ritual purification, if they can afford to do so. No matter how ill the supplicant or how grave the emergency, the guardians of many temples will not admit a client if he cannot give a rich gift to the custodian. Even after one has gained admission and survived the ceremonies, the guardians will not permit the neophyte to leave until he makes still another gift.

The supplicant entering the temple is first stripped of all his or her clothes. In every-day life the Nacirema avoids exposure of his body and its natural functions. Bathing and excretory acts are performed only in the secrecy of the household shrine, where they are ritualized as part of the body-rites. Psychological shock results from the fact that body secrecy is suddenly lost upon entry into the *lati pso*. A man, whose own wife has never seen him in an excretory act, suddenly finds himself naked and assisted by a vestal maiden while he performs his natural functions into a sacred vessel. This sort of ceremonial treatment is necessitated by the fact that the excreta are used by a diviner to ascertain the course and nature of the client's sickness. Female clients, on the other hand, find their naked bodies are subjected to the scrutiny, manipulation and prodding of the medicine men.

There remains one other kind of practitioner, known as the "listener." This witch-doctor has the power to exorcise the devils that lodge in the heads of people who have been bewitched. The Nacirema believe that parents bewitch their own children. Mothers are particularly suspected of putting a curse on children while teaching them the sacred body rituals. The patient simply tells the "listener" all his troubles and fears, beginning with the earliest difficulties he can remember. The memory displayed by the Nacirema in these exorcism sessions is truly remarkable. It is not uncommon for the patient to bemoan the rejection he felt upon being weaned as a babe, and a few individuals even see their troubles going back to the traumatic effects of their own birth.

In conclusion, mention must be made of certain practices which have their base in native esthetics but which depend upon the pervasive aversion to the natural body and its functions. There are ritual fasts to make fat people thin and ceremonial feast to make thin people fat. Still other rites are used to make women's breasts larger if they are small and smaller if they are large. General dissatisfaction with breast shape is symbolized in the fact that the ideal form is virtually outside the range of human variation. A few women afflicted with almost inhuman hyper-mammary development are so idolized that they make a handsome living by simply going from village to village and permitting the natives to stare at them for a fee.

Reference has already been made to the fact that excretory functions are ritualized, routinized, and relegated to secrecy. Natural reproductive functions are similarly distorted. Intercourse is taboo as a topic and scheduled as an act. Efforts are made to avoid pregnancy by the use of magical materials or by limiting intercourse to certain phases of the moon. Conception is actually very infrequent. When pregnant, women dress so as to hide their condition. Parturition takes place in secret, without friends or relatives to assist, and the majority of women do not nurse their infants.

Our review of the ritual life of the Nacirema has certainly shown them to be a magic-ridden people. It is hard to understand how they have managed to exist so long under the burdens which they have imposed upon themselves. But even such exotic customs as these take on real meaning when they are viewed with the insight provided by Malinowski when he wrote (1948:70):

> Looking from far and above, from our high places of safety in the developed civilization, it is easy to see all the crudity and irrelevance of magic. But without its power and guidance early man could not have mastered his practical difficulties as he has done, nor could man have advanced to the higher stages of civilization.

References Cited

Lenton, Ralph; 1936, *The Study of Man*. New York, D. Appleton-Century Co.

Malinowski, Bronislaw; 1948, *Magic, Science, and Religion*. Glencoe, The Free Press.

Murdock, George P.; 1949, *Social Structure*. New York, The Macmillan Co.

1. What is your opinion of the importance of body ritual? If you lived among the Nacirema, would you tell them of your opinion? To what extent can you identify with the article?

2. Compare and contrast the rituals of the Nacirema with some of your own body rituals.

3. Write "Nacirema" backwards. In small groups, discuss your reactions to this article and its implications.

Journalist Jane Flanagan writes for the South African bureau of the British news source The Telegraph. *Her articles and reports often appear on the news source's online version at www.telegraph.co.uk.*

DRUNK BABOONS PLAGUE CAPE TOWN'S EXCLUSIVE SUBURBS

By Jane Flanagan

Groot Constantia, in the heart of Cape Town's wine country, can deal with inebriated holidaymakers—but it is invading baboons which have developed a taste for its grapes that the wine makers are struggling with.

Each day, dozens of Cape Baboons gather to strip the ancient vines—the sauvignon blanc grapes are a particular favourite—before heading into the mountains to sleep. A few, who sample fallen fruit that has fermented in the sun, pass out and don't make it home.

"They are not just eating our grapes, they are raiding our kitchens and ripping the thatch off the roofs. They are becoming increasingly bold and destructive," said Jean Naude, general manager at the vineyard, which is celebrating its 325th birthday this year. Guards banging sticks and waving plastic snakes have been deployed with only limited success, and not even a blast of a vuvuzela, the plastic horn made famous at the World Cup, seems to frighten them.

It is not just the vineyards in South Africa which are under siege, however, but also the exclusive neighbouring suburb of Constantia, home to famous residents including Earl Spencer, Wilbur Smith, and Nelson Mandela.

Crisis meetings between animal welfare groups and traumatised locals are struggling to find a workable solution.

"Where there's a mountain, there's a baboon," said Justin O'Riain of the Baboon Research Unit at the University of Cape Town. "As we take up more and more of their land, the conflict increases."

The baboons lived in the mountains of Cape Town long before humans took up residence, but development has forced the unlikely neighbours into increasingly closer contact.

Before laws afforded baboons a protected status a decade ago, troublesome animals were regularly killed or maimed by home owners and farmers. Now around 20 full-time "baboon monitors" are employed to protect them and guide them away from residential areas. It has proved mission impossible. Last week, a 12-year-old boy was left traumatised after confronting a troop who had broken into his family home.

Hearing noises from the kitchen, he went to investigate and found the beasts ransacking cupboards. When the child fled upstairs to find his babysitter, three males gave chase and surrounded him as he made a tearful phone call to his mother, while the animals pelted him with fruit.

"When he called me he was terrified. They had him surrounded," said the Constantia housewife, who did not wish to be identified.

Chickens, geese, peacocks and even a Great Dane dog have been killed in recent weeks by the marauding baboons—the males have huge and terrifying canine teeth. Roof tiles, electric fences, orchards and vegetables gardens have been trashed.

"Lunch parties in the garden are now just impossible," a homeowner complained. "It is so unrelaxing. Rather than chatting over our meal, we are looking over our shoulders and bolting the food as quickly as we can before it is stolen. We can't even leave a window open in summer. We are under siege."

In a concession to despairing residents, wildlife authorities have begun collaring baboons identified as "troublesome" and imposed a strict "three strikes" policy whereby animals which repeatedly break into homes are humanely destroyed.

Fourteen year-old William, a large male known officially as GOB03, who had terrorised the coastal suburb of Scarborough for as long as anyone can remember, was the first to fall foul of this controversial rule.

His death last month was greeted with outrage and jubilation in equal measure and dominated the letters pages of the local newspapers for weeks.

Meanwhile, For Sale signs are sprouting up in suburbs with baboon populations. Families which have lived in the same house for generations are giving up, moving away to get away from their animal tormentors.

Initially the title of this article may sound amusing, but in reality it is a serious issue. Whose rights should take precedence, "Families (human property rights) which have lived in the same house for generations" or Baboons (Animal rights) who lived in the mountains "long before humans took up residence"?

The article mentions that "the exclusive neighbouring suburb of Constantia, home to famous residents including...Nelson Mandela" is under attack. Why is this information important? How might this impact the local and/or global economics?

How do you, an American, connect with this story from across the world? Think about all of the elements in this story that may be similar and those that are different. What inferences can you make from this that may impact your life? Your future world?

Think about how the rhetoric of the article contributes to your reaction after your first reading. Now, read it again. How does the rhetoric affect you? Is there a difference? Are some voices more emotionally effective? Are some more logically effective?

This article was originally published on August 30, 2010 in the weekly satirical newspaper The Onion. The Onion *parodies current political events and social issues in the United States.*

MAN ALREADY KNOWS EVERYTHING HE NEEDS TO KNOW ABOUT MUSLIMS

BY THE ONION

MAN ALREADY KNOWS EVERYTHING HE NEEDS TO KNOW ABOUT MUSLIMS

SALINA, KS—Local man Scott Gentries told reporters Wednesday that his deliberately limited grasp of Islamic history and culture was still more than sufficient to shape his views of the entire Muslim world.

Gentries, 48, said he had absolutely no interest in exposing himself to further knowledge of Islamic civilization or putting his sweeping opinions into a broader context of any kind, and confirmed he was "perfectly happy" to make a handful of emotionally charged words the basis of his mistrust toward all members of the world's second-largest religion.

"I learned all that really matters about the Muslim faith on 9/11," Gentries said in reference to the terrorist attacks on the United States undertaken by 19 of Islam's approximately 1.6 billion practitioners. "What more do I need to know to stigmatize Muslims everywhere as inherently violent radicals?"

"And now they want to build a mosque at Ground Zero," continued Gentries, eliminating any distinction between the 9/11 hijackers and Muslims in general. "No, I won't examine the accuracy of that statement, but yes, I will allow myself to be outraged by it and use it as evidence of these people's universal callousness toward Americans who lost loved ones when the Twin Towers fell."

"Even though I am not one of those people," he added.

When told that the proposed "Ground Zero mosque" is actually a community center two blocks north of the site that would include, in addition to a public prayer space, a 500-seat auditorium, a restaurant, and athletic facilities, Gentries shook his head and said, "I know all I'm going to let myself know."

Gentries explained that it "didn't take long" to find out as much about the tenets of Islam as he needed to. He said he knew Muslims stoned their women for committing adultery, trained for terrorist attacks at fundamentalist madrassas, and believed in jihad, which Gentries described as the thing they used to justify killing infidels.

"All Muslims are at war with America, and I will resist any attempt to challenge that assertion with potentially illuminating facts," said Gentries, who threatened to leave the room if presented with the number of Muslims who live peacefully in the United States, serve in the country's armed forces, or were victims themselves of the 9/11 attacks. "Period."

"If you don't believe me, wait until they put your wife in a burka," Gentries continued in reference to the face-and-body-covering worn by a small minority of Muslim women and banned in the universities of Turkey, Tunisia, and Syria. "Or worse, a rape camp. That's right: For reasons I am content being totally unable to articulate, I am choosing to associate Muslims with rape camps."

Over the past decade, Gentries said he has taken pains to avoid personal interactions or media that might have the potential to compromise his point of view. He told reporters that the closest he had come to confronting a contrary standpoint was tuning in to the first few seconds of an interview with a moderate Muslim cleric before hastily turning off the television.

"I almost gave in and listened to that guy defend Islam with words I didn't want to hear," Gentries said. "But then I remembered how much easier it is to live in a world of black-and-white in which I can assign the label of 'other' to someone and use him as a vessel for all my fears and insecurities."

Added Gentries, "That really put things back into perspective."

1. According to Gentries, all Muslims believe in jihad, which he describes as "the thing [Muslims] use to justify killing infidels." The authors of *The Onion* are aware that this is one potential perspective that people may have, but does that mean that this version of jihad is true? Research the concept of jihad. What is it? According to whom?

2. "For reasons I am content being totally unable to articulate, I am choosing to associate Muslims with rape camps." –Gentries

   Do you think it is necessary for a person's credibility as a speaker or writer to be able to provide evidence to support his or her beliefs? Why? What kinds of evidence are needed?

3. In what ways does this article resemble an actual newspaper article? In what ways does it differ? Why do you think the authors would try to recreate the tone of a newspaper article for this spoof?

Azar Nafisi, born in 1955, is a scholarly writer and former professor. After receiving her Ph.D. in Literature from the University of Oklahoma, Nafisi returned to her native Iran and taught at multiple universities. In 1997, she and her family emigrated to the United States, and she began writing her memoir of times teaching and leading a book club of women. Reading Lolita in Tehran, published in 2003, was on the New York Times bestsellers list for over two years and received both praise and criticism for Nafisi's portrayal of life in Iran.

READING *LOLITA* IN TEHRAN

BY AZAR NAFISI

In the fall of 1995, after resigning from my last academic post, I decided to indulge myself and fulfill a dream. I chose seven of my best and most committed students and invited them to come to my home every Thursday morning to discuss literature. They were all women— to teach a mixed class in the privacy of my home was too risky, even if we were discussing harmless works of fiction. One persistent male student, although barred from our class, insisted on his rights. So he, Nima, read the assigned material, and on special days he would come to my house to talk about the books we were reading.

I often teasingly reminded my students of Muriel Spark's *The Prime of Miss Jean Brodie* and asked, Which one of you will finally betray me? For I am a pessimist by nature, and I was sure at least one would turn against me. Nassrin once responded mischievously, "You yourself told us that in the final analysis we are our own betrayers, playing Judas to our own Christ." Manna pointed out that I was no Miss Brodie, and they, well, they were what they were. She reminded me of a warning I was fond of repeating: *do not*, under *any* circumstances, belittle a work of fiction by trying to turn it into a carbon copy of real life; what we search for in fiction is not so much reality but the epiphany of truth. Yet I suppose that if I were to go against my own recommendation and choose a work of fiction that would most resonate with our lives in the Islamic Republic of Iran, it would not be *The Prime of Miss Jean Brodie* or even *1984* but perhaps Nabokov's *Invitation to a Beheading* or better yet, *Lolita*.

A couple of years after we had begun our Thursday morning seminars, on the last night I was in Tehran, a few friends and students came to say good-bye and to help me pack. When we had deprived the house of all its items, when the objects had vanished and the colors had faded into eight gray suitcases, like errant genies evaporating into their bottles, my students and I stood against the bare white wall of the dining room and took two photographs.

I have the two photographs in front of me now. In the first there are seven women, standing against a white wall. They are, according to the law of the land, dressed in black robes and head scarves, covered except for the oval of their faces and their hands. In the second photograph the same group, in the same position, stands against the same wall. Only they have taken off their coverings. Splashes of color separate one from the next. Each has become distinct through the color and style of her clothes, the color and the length of her hair; not even the two who are still wearing their head scarves look the same.

The one to the far right in the second photograph is our poet, Manna, in a white T-shirt and jeans. She made poetry out of things most people cast aside. The photograph does not reflect the peculiar opacity of Manna's dark eyes, a testament to her withdrawn and private nature.

Next to Manna is Mahshid, whose long black scarf clashes with her delicate features and retreating smile. Mahshid was good at many things, but she had a certain daintiness about her and we took to calling her "my lady." Nassrin used to say that more than defining Mahshid, we had managed to add another dimension to the word *lady*. Mahshid is very sensitive. She's like porcelain, Yassi once told me, easy to crack. That's why she appears fragile to those who don't know her too well; but woe to whoever offends her. As for me, Yassi continued good-naturedly, I'm like good old plastic; I won't crack no matter what you do with me.

Yassi was the youngest in our group. She is the one in yellow, bending forward and bursting with laughter. We used to teasingly call her our comedian. Yassi was shy by nature, but certain things excited her and made her lose her inhibitions. She had a tone of voice that gently mocked and questioned not just others but herself as well.

I am the one in brown, standing next to Yassi, with one arm around her shoulders. Directly behind me stands Azin, my tallest student, with her long blond hair and a pink T-shirt. She is laughing like the rest of us. Azin's smiles never looked like smiles; they appeared more like preludes to an irrepressible and nervous hilarity. She beamed in that peculiar fashion even when she was describing her latest trouble with her husband. Always outrageous and outspoken, Azin relished the shock value of her actions and comments and often clashed with Mahshid and Manna. We nicknamed her the wild one.

On my other side is Mitra, who was perhaps the calmest among us. Like the pastel colors of her paintings, she seemed to recede and fade into a paler register. Her beauty was saved from predictability by a pair of miraculous dimples, which she could and did use to manipulate any an unsuspecting victim into bending to her will.

Sanaz, who, pressured by family and society, vacillated between her desire for independence and her need for approval, is holding on to Mitra's arm. We are all laughing. And Nima, Manna's husband and my one true literary critic—if only he had had the perseverance to finish the brilliant essays he started to write—is our invisible partner, the photographer.

There was one more: Nassrin. She is not in the photographs—she didn't make it to the end. Yet my tale would be incomplete without those who could not or did not remain with us. Their absences persist, like an acute pain that seems to have no physical source. This is Tehran for me: its absences were more real than its presences.

When I see Nassrin in my mind's eye, she's slightly out of focus, blurred, somehow distant. I've combed through the photographs my students took with me over the years, and Nassrin is in many of them but always hidden behind something—a person, a tree. In one,

I am standing with eight of my students in the small garden facing our faculty building, the scene of so many farewell photographs over the years. In the background stands a sheltering willow tree. We are laughing, and in one corner, from behind the tallest student, Nassrin peers out, like an imp intruding roguishly on a scene it was not invited to. In another I can barely make out her face in the small V space behind two other girls' shoulders. In this one she looks absentminded; she is frowning, as if unaware that she is being photographed.

How can I describe Nassrin? I once called her the Cheshire cat, appearing and disappearing at unexpected turns in my academic life. The truth is I can't describe her: she was her own definition. One can only say that Nassrin was Nassrin.

For nearly two years, almost every Thursday morning, rain or shine, they came to my house, and almost every time, I could not get over the shock of seeing them shed their mandatory veils and robes and burst into color. When my students came into that room, they took off more than their scarves and robes. Gradually, each one gained an outline and a shape, becoming her own inimitable self. Our world in that living room with its window framing my beloved Elburz Mountains became our sanctuary, our self-contained universe, mocking the reality of black-scarved, timid faces in the city that sprawled below.

The theme of the class was the relation between fiction and reality. We read Persian classical literature, such as the tales of our own lady of fiction, Scheherazade, from *A Thousand and One Nights*, along with Western classics—*Pride and Prejudice, Madame Bovary, Daisy Miller, The Dean's December* and, yes, *Lolita*. As I write the title of each book, memories whirl in with the wind to disturb the quiet of this fall day in another room in another country.

Here and now in that other world that cropped up so many times in our discussions, I sit and reimagine myself and my students, my girls as I came to call them, reading *Lolita* in a deceptively sunny room in Tehran. But to steal the words from Humbert, the poet/criminal of *Lolita*, I need you, the reader, to imagine us, for we won't really exist if you don't. Against the tyranny of time and politics, imagine us the way we sometimes didn't dare to imagine ourselves: in our most private and secret moments, in the most extraordinarily ordinary instances of life, listening to music, falling in love, walking down the shady streets or reading *Lolita* in Tehran. And then imagine us again with all this confiscated, driven underground, taken away from us.

If I write about Nabokov today, it is to celebrate our reading of Nabokov in Tehran, against all odds. Of all his novels I choose the one I taught last, and the one that is connected to so many memories. It is of Lolita that I want to write, but right now there is no way I can write about that novel without also writing about Tehran. This, then, is the story of *Lolita* in Tehran, how *Lolita* gave a different color to Tehran and how Tehran helped redefine Nabokov's novel, turning it into this *Lolita*, our *Lolita*.

1. In the first chapter of the book, Nafisi writes about a conversation that questions the differences between fiction and reality. How is this discussion similar to the one about actual versus perceived culture?

2. If you were under a regime such as the one in the book that restricted learning, would your education have continued to flourish? Is such a desire for knowledge irrepressible?

3. How powerful is clothing in a culture?

Heather Carreiro, English Department Head at the International School of Ho Chi Minh City's American Academy, while teaching English, works as a freelance writer. She has contributed to Matador Network, BootsnAll, GoNOMAD, and Journey Beyond Travel. In addition to teaching in Vietnam, she spent three years teaching and developing English language courses in Pakistan.

DEFINITIONS OF MODESTY: BIKINIS IN THE SUPERMARKET, BURKINIS AT THE POOL

By Heather Carreiro

Does any culture have the right to define modesty, nudity or "freedom" for everyone else?

In the wake of Facebook's decision to remove photos of women breastfeeding, a lively debate sparked on *Matador Life* about cultural perceptions of breastfeeding, misogynistic attitudes toward women's bodies and the definition of pornography.

This led to the questioning of our definitions of concepts like "modesty" and "nudity." Is there a universal standard of what should be considered modest or lewd? If one culture considers showing certain body parts as public nudity while another does not, does the second culture have the right to see the first as backward, oppressive or uneducated because of its differing views of modesty?

There are organizations, such as the Topfree Equal Rights Society (TERA), that promote the legal right for women be topless in public places. The TERA website states, "We do believe that since men may choose to do so [go topless] in many situations, women must also be able to at least in the same situations. Without penalty of any kind."

TERA questions the premise of what is defined legally as nudity and why women who go topless are often considered to be in violation of public decency laws while men who go topless are not. While TERA focuses only on the United States and Canada, the existence of organizations like TERA, along with the following examples, make me wonder what the limitations are when it comes to determining what is a 'right'; what is a violation of other people's rights, and if it is even possible to agree to national or universal standards when it comes to issues like modesty and public nudity.

BIKINIS IN THE SUPERMARKET, BURKINIS AT THE POOL

In the U.S. it is common to see cleavage in public and skimpy bathing suits on the beach, but why is it that if a woman showed up in a bikini in the supermarket she would elicit stares? What if a man went to his office wearing only boxer shorts?

In American culture it is generally not acceptable to expose that amount of skin in public. A woman in a matching g-string and a bra could not go to the neighborhood ATM without being noticed, yet if she happened to be standing on sand or near a body of water nobody would blink an eye. Well, unless of course they were checking her out.

Even in current-day Western culture, we can see that there are no clear lines. What is modest at the beach is immodest at the workplace. We have different standards of what is appropriate and inappropriate based on different contexts.

In some cases it can even be taboo to wear too much clothing. Just this month a French Muslim woman was banned from a public swimming pool in Paris. Her crime: having too much skin covered. She showed up wearing a burkini, a wetsuit-like garment that also covers the hair. Not only was she prevented from swimming with her children, but a local government official deemed her decision to wear the suit as "obviously a provocation by a militant."

In France right now, there is significant debate over whether the burka should be banned. French President Sarkozy has made it clear that "the burka is not welcome in France" and has called it "a sign of subservience…a sign of lowering."

The question here is: Is it naïve to assume that all women who wear a burka or burkini are oppressed? Should we completely discount the idea that some of these women choose to wear such garments from their own personal conviction or preference, whether or not similar garments serve as a sign of oppression for other women?

Just as most of us in the West would feel embarrassed if we were stripped to our underwear in public, could it not be that some of these women simply feel uncomfortable and shamed at the thought of showing their legs, knees, or even their faces?

NAKED BRITNEY SPEARS

In Japan, posters of a pregnant, naked Britney Spears were temporarily banned from subway stations. The poster portrayed the cover of *Harper's Bazaar* August 2006 magazine issue, and at the time many Western bloggers criticized Japanese officials for being prude and not promoting the beauty of a pregnant female body.

Eventually the subway company caved and ran the ad, but if other nude ads similar to the Spears photo had been rejected in the past, why should the fact that the singer was pregnant force the company to treat the Spears ad differently? A spokesman for Toyko Metro explained that, "Our earlier request to cover the photo from the waist down was because of nudity, not because we had anything against pregnant women."

This is an example of how one culture, represented by the editorial team at *Harper's Bazaar*, did not take into account the norms of another culture regarding what constitutes public nudity. Just because we may not be phased seeing a naked singer on billboards or magazine covers, does that mean other cultures should be forced to get used to it too?

MINI-SKIRTS, CAR ACCIDENTS AND GUERILLA WARFARE

In response to a 1970 mini-skirt ban in Malawi, one European expat wrote about how the country's "paradise was shattered" due to the ban, and it was now "a question of guerilla warfare. Chins up, hems up is the order of the day." The article relates stories of expat women ignoring the ban, getting deported for breaking the mini-skirt rule and conspiring ways to get around it.

Throughout southern Africa, the waist, hips and butt are often seen as the most sexual part of a woman's body. Countrywide mini-skirts bans have also been enacted in Swaziland and Uganda after an increase in traffic accidents allegedly caused by immodestly dressed woman. Mini-skirt wearers, both locals and foreigners, have been accused of indecency and public nudity.

Something makes me question the ethnocentrism of the European expat's attitude toward the Malawi mini-skirt ban. It is really our place to engage in "guerilla warfare" against another culture's concept of modesty? Glimpse contributor Saman Maydani wrestled with a similar issue when it came to wearing pants in Zambia. After a local man shared with her that wearing pants was considered to be "morally degenerative," she chose a different course of action than the expat women in Malawi. She started wearing skirts.

In the West, we sometimes hold to this ideas that less clothing inherently equals more freedom, and that any culture that promotes differing views of modesty is either behind the times, fundamentalist or oppressive. I see the situation as much more complicated than that, and to assume to that our view of what modesty is defines freedom or lack of it just serves as another face of cultural imperialism.

1. How do you define modesty? What cultural ideals, such as religion or nationality, affect your definition? Could your definition be considered wrong by a different culture? Why?

2. Many countries, France especially, are accusing women of being too modest and promoting an oppressive culture. Do you agree that one can be "too modest?" Can modesty be oppressive?

Arlie Russell Hochschild is a Professor Emerita of Sociology at The University of California at Berkeley. She has received the Lifetime Achievement Award from the American Sociological Association for her pioneering work in the Sociology of Emotions. Her most recent book, The Outsourced Self: Intimate Life in Market Time, was chosen as one of Publisher's Weekly's Best Books of 2012.

THE NANNY CHAIN

BY ARLIE RUSSELL HOCHSCHILD

Vicky Diaz, a 34-year-old mother of five, was a college-educated schoolteacher and travel agent in the Philippines before migrating to the United States to work as a housekeeper for a wealthy Beverly Hills family and as a nanny for their two-year-old son. Her children, Vicky explained to Rhacel Parrenas,

> were saddened by my departure. Even until now my children are trying to convince me to go home. The children were not angry when I left because they were still very young when I left them. My husband could not get angry either because he knew that was the only way I could seriously help him raise our children, so that our children could be sent to school. I send them money every month.

In her forthcoming book *Servants of Globalization*, Parrenas, an affiliate of the Center for Working Families at the University of California, Berkeley, tells an important and disquieting story of what she calls the "globalization of mothering." The Beverly Hills family pays "Vicky" (which is the pseudonym Parrenas gave her) $400 a week, and Vicky, in turn, pays her own family's live-in domestic worker back in the Philippines $40 a week. Living like this is not easy on Vicky and her family. "Even though it's paid well, you are sinking in the amount of your work. Even while you are ironing the clothes, they can still call you to the kitchen to wash the plates. It ... [is] also very depressing. The only thing you can do is give all your love to [the two-year-old American child]. In my absence from my children, the most I could do with my situation is give all my love to that child."

Vicky is part of what we could call a *global care chain*: a series of personal links between people across the globe based on the paid or unpaid work of caring. A typical global care chain might work something like this: An older daughter from a poor family in a third world country cares for her siblings (the first link in the chain) while her mother works as a nanny caring for the children of a nanny migrating to a first world country (the second link) who, in turn, cares for the child of a family in a rich country (the final link). Each kind of chain expresses an invisible human *ecology of care*, one care worker depending on another and so on. A global care chain might start in a poor country and end in a rich one, or it might link rural and urban areas within the same poor country. More complex versions start in one poor country and extend to another slightly less poor country and then link to a rich country.

Global care chains may be proliferating. According to 1994 estimates by the International Organization for Migration, 120 million people migrated legally or illegally from one country to another. That's two percent of the world's population. How many migrants leave loved ones behind to care for other peoples' children or elderly parents, we don't know. But we do know that more than half of legal migrants to the United States are women, mostly between ages 25 and 34. And migration experts tell us that the proportion of women among migrants is likely to rise. All of this suggests that the trend toward global care chains will continue.

How are we to understand the impact of globalization on care? If, as globalization continues, more global care chains form, will they be "good" care chains or "bad" ones? Given the entrenched problem of third world poverty, which is one of the starting points for care chains, this is by no means a simple question. But we have yet to fully address it, I believe, because the world is globalizing faster than our minds or hearts are. We live global but still think and feel local.

FREUD IN A GLOBAL ECONOMY

Most writing on globalization focuses on money, markets, and labor flows, while giving scant attention to women, children, and the care of one for the other. Most research on women and development, meanwhile, draws a connection between, say, World Bank loan conditions and the scarcity of food for women and children in the third world, without saying much about resources expended on caregiving. Much of the research on women in the United States and Europe focuses on a chainless, two-person picture of "work-family balance" without considering the child care worker and the emotional ecology of which he or she is a part. Fortunately, in recent years, scholars such as Ernestine Avila, Evelyn Nakano Glenn, Pierette Hondagneu-Sotelo, Mary Romero, and Rhacel Parrenas have produced some fascinating research on domestic workers. Building on this work, we can begin to focus on the first world end of the care chain and begin spelling out some of the implications of the globalization of love.

One difficulty in understanding these implications is that the language of economics does not translate easily into the language of psychology. How are we to understand a "transfer" of feeling from one link in a chain to another? Feeling is not a "resource" that can be crassly taken from one person and given to another. And surely one person can love quite a few people; love is not a resource limited the same way oil or currency supply is. Or is it?

Consider Sigmund Freud's theory of displacement, the idea that emotion can be redirected from one person or object to another. Freud believed that if, for example, Jane loves Dick but Dick is emotionally or literally unavailable, Jane will find a new object (say, John, Dick and Jane's son) onto which to project her original feeling for Dick. While Freud applied the idea of displacement mainly to relations within the nuclear family, the concept can also be applied to relations extending far outside it. For example, immigrant nannies and au pairs often divert feelings originally directed toward their own children toward their young charges in this country. As Sauling C. Wong, a researcher at the University of California, Berkeley, has put it, "Time and energy available for mothers are diverted from those who, by kinship or communal ties, are their more rightful recipients."

If it is true that attention, solicitude, and love itself can be "displaced" from one child (let's say Vicky Diaz's son Alfredo, back in the Philippines) onto another child (let's say Tommy, the son of her employers in Beverly Hills), then the important observation to make here is that this displacement is often upward in wealth and power. This, in turn, raises the question of the equitable distribution of care. It makes us wonder, is there in the realm of love an analogue to what Marx calls "surplus value," something skimmed off from the poor for the benefit of the rich?

Seen as a thing in itself, Vicky's love for the Beverly Hills toddler is unique, individual, private. But might there not be elements in this love that are borrowed, so to speak, from somewhere and someone else? Is time spent with the first world child in some sense "taken" from a child further down the care chain? Is the Beverly Hills child getting "surplus" love, the way immigrant farm workers give us surplus labor? Are first world countries such as the United States importing maternal love as they have imported copper, zinc, gold, and other ores from third world countries in the past?

This is a startling idea and an unwelcome one, both for Vicky Diaz, who needs the money from a first world job, and for her well-meaning employers, who want someone to give loving care to their child. Each link in the chain feels she is doing the right thing for good reasons, and who is to say she is not?

But there are clearly hidden costs here, costs that tend to get passed down along the chain. One nanny reported such a cost when she described (to Rhacel Parrenas) a return visit to the Philippines: "When I saw my children, I thought, 'Oh children do grow up even without their mother.' I left my youngest when she was only five years old. She was already nine when I saw her again but she still wanted for me to carry her [weeps]. That hurt me because it showed me that my children missed out on a lot."

Sometimes the toll it takes on the domestic worker is overwhelming and suggests that the nanny has not displaced her love onto an employer's child but rather has continued to long intensely for her own child. As one woman told Parrenas, "The first two years I felt like I was going crazy. . . . I would catch myself gazing at nothing, thinking about my child. Every moment, every second of the day, I felt like I was thinking about my baby. My youngest, you have to understand, I left when he was only two months old. . . . You know, whenever I receive a letter from my children, I cannot sleep. I cry. It's good that my job is more demanding at night."

Despite the anguish these separations clearly cause, Filipina women continue to leave for jobs abroad. Since the early 1990s, 55 percent of migrants out of the Philippines have been women; next to electronic manufacturing, their remittances make up the major source of foreign currency in the Philippines. The rate of female emigration has continued to increase and includes college-educated teachers, businesswomen, and secretaries. In Parrenas's study, more than half of the nannies she interviewed had college degrees and most were married mothers in their 30s.

Here are men in this picture? For the most part, men especially men at the top of the class ladder leave child-rearing to women. Many of the husbands and fathers of Parrenas's domestic workers had migrated to the Arabian peninsula and other places in search of better wages, relieving other men of "male work" as construction workers and tradesmen, while being replaced themselves at home. Others remained at home, responsible fathers caring or helping to care for their children. But some of the men tyrannized their wives. Indeed, many of the women migrants Parrenas interviewed didn't just leave; they fled. As one migrant maid explained:

> You have to understand that my problems were very heavy before I left the Philippines. My husband was abusive. I couldn't even think about my children, the only thing I could think about was the opportunity to escape my situation. If my husband was not going to kill me, I was probably going to kill him... . He always beat me up and my parents wanted me to leave him for a long time. I left my children with my sister... . In the plane ... I felt like a bird whose cage had been locked for many years... . I felt free... . Deep inside, I felt homesick for my children but I also felt free for being able to escape the most dire problem that was slowly killing me.

Other men abandoned their wives. A former public school teacher back in the Philippines confided to Parrenas: "After three years of marriage, my husband left me for another woman. My husband supported us for just a little over a year. Then the support was stopped. . . . The letters stopped. I have not seen him since." In the absence of government aid, then, migration becomes a way of coping with abandonment.

Sometimes the husband of a female migrant worker is himself a migrant worker who takes turns with his wife migrating. One Filipino man worked in Saudi Arabia for 10 years, coming home for a month each year. When he finally returned home for good, his wife set off to work as a maid in America while he took care of the children. As she explained to Parrenas, "My children were very sad when I left them. My husband told me that when they came back home from the airport, my children could not touch their food and they wanted to cry. My son, whenever he writes me, always draws the head of Fido the dog with tears on the eyes. Whenever he goes to Mass on Sundays, he tells me that he misses me more because he sees his friends with their mothers. Then he comes home and cries."

THE END OF THE CHAIN

Just as global capitalism helps create a third world supply of mothering, it creates a first world demand for it. The past half-century has witnessed a huge rise in the number of women in paid work from 15 percent of mothers of children aged 6 and under in 1950 to 65 percent today. Indeed, American women now make up 45 percent of the American labor force. Three-quarters of mothers of children 18 and under now work, as do 65 percent of mothers of children 6 and under. In addition, a recent report by the International Labor Organization reveals that the average number of hours of work per week has been rising in this country.

Earlier generations of American working women would rely on grandmothers and other female kin to help look after their children; now the grandmothers and aunts are themselves busy doing paid work outside the home. Statistics show that over the past 30 years a decreasing number of families have relied on relatives to care for their children and hence are compelled to look for nonfamily care. At the first world end of care chains, working parents are grateful to find a good nanny or child care provider, and they are generally able to pay far more than the nanny could earn in her native country. This is not just a child care problem. Many American families are now relying on immigrant or out-of-home care for their *elderly* relatives. As a Los Angeles elder-care worker, an immigrant, told Parrenas, "Domestics here are able to make a living from the elderly that families abandon." But this often means that nannies cannot take care of their own ailing parents and therefore produce an elder-care version of a child care chain caring for first world elderly persons while a paid worker cares for their aged mother back in the Philippines.

My own research for two books, *The Second Shift* and *The Time Bind*, sheds some light on the first world end of the chain. Many women have joined the law, academia, medicine, business but such professions are still organized for men who are free of family responsibilities. The successful career, at least for those who are broadly middle class or above, is still largely built on some key traditional components: doing professional work, competing with fellow professionals, getting credit for work, building a reputation while you're young, hoarding scarce time, and minimizing family obligations by finding someone else to deal with domestic chores. In the past, the professional was a man and the "someone else to deal with [chores]" was a wife. The wife oversaw the family, which in pre-industrial times, anyway, was supposed to absorb the human vicissitudes of birth, sickness, and death that the workplace discarded. Today, men take on much more of the child care and housework at home, but they still base their identity on demanding careers in the context of which children are beloved impediments; hence, men resist sharing care equally at home. So when parents don't have enough "caring time" between them, they feel forced to look for that care further down the global chain.

The ultimate beneficiaries of these various care changes might actually be large multinational companies, usually based in the United States. In my research on a Fortune 500 manufacturing company I call Amerco, I discovered a disproportionate number of women employed in the human side of the company: public relations, marketing, human resources. In all sectors of the company, women often helped others sort out problems both personal and professional at work. It was often the welcoming voice and "soft touch" of women workers that made Amerco seem like a family to other workers. In other words, it appears that these working mothers displace some of their emotional labor from their children to their employer, which holds itself out to the worker as a "family." So, the care in the chain may begin with that which a rural third world mother gives (as a nanny) the urban child she cares for, and it may end with the care a working mother gives her employees as the vice president of publicity at your company.

HOW MUCH IS CARE WORTH?

How are we to respond to the growing number of global care chains? Through what perspective should we view them?

I can think of three vantage points from which to see care chains: that of the primordialist, the sunshine modernist, and (my own) the critical modernist. The primordialist believes that our primary responsibility is to our own family, our own community, our own country. According to this view, if we all tend our own primordial plots, everybody will be fine. There is some logic to this point of view. After all, Freud's concept of displacement rests on the premise that some original first object of love has a primary "right" to that love, and second and third comers don't fully share that right. (For the primordialist as for most all of us those first objects are members of one's most immediate family.) But the primordialist is an isolationist, an antiglobalist. To such a person, care chains seem wrong not because they're unfair to the least-cared-for children at the bottom of the chain, but because they are global. Also, because family care has historically been provided by women, primordialists often believe that women should stay home to provide this care.

The sunshine modernist, on the other hand, believes care chains are just fine, an inevitable part of globalization, which is itself uncritically accepted as good. The idea of displacement is hard for the sunshine modernists to grasp because in their equation seen mainly in economic terms the global market will sort out who has proper claims on a nanny's love. As long as the global supply of labor meets the global demand for it, the sunshine modernist believes, everything will be okay.

If the primordialist thinks care chains are bad because they're global, the sunshine modernist thinks they're good for the very same reason. In either case, the issue of inequality of access to care disappears.

The critical modernist embraces modernity but with a global sense of ethics. When the critical modernist goes out to buy a pair of Nike shoes, she is concerned to learn how low the wage was and how long the hours were for the third world factory worker making the shoes. The critical modernist applies the same moral concern to care chains: The welfare of the Filipino child back home must be seen as some part, however small, of the total picture. The critical modernist sees globalization as a very mixed blessing, bringing with it new opportunities such as the nanny's access to good wages but also new problems, including emotional and psychological costs we have hardly begun to understand.

From the critical modernist perspective, globalization may be increasing inequities not simply in access to money and those inequities are important enough but in access to care. The poor maid's child may be getting less motherly care than the first world child. (And for that matter, because of longer hours of work, the first world child may not be getting the ideal quantity of parenting attention for healthy development because too much of it is now displaced onto the employees of Fortune 500 companies.) We needn't lapse into primordialism to sense that something may be amiss in this.

I see no easy solutions to the human costs of global care chains. But here are some initial thoughts. We might, for example, reduce the incentive to migrate by addressing the causes of the migrant's economic desperation and fostering economic growth in the third world. Thus one obvious goal would be to develop the Filipino economy.

But it's not so simple. Immigration scholars have demonstrated that development itself can *encourage* migration because development gives rise to new economic uncertainties that families try to mitigate by seeking employment in the first world. If members of a family are laid off at home, a migrant's monthly remittance can see them through, often by making a capital outlay in a small business or paying for a child's education.

Other solutions might focus on individual links in the care chain. Because some women migrate to flee abusive husbands, a partial solution would be to create local refuges from such husbands. Another would be to alter immigration policy so as to encourage nannies to bring their children with them. Alternatively, employers or even government subsidies could help nannies make regular visits home.

The most fundamental approach to the problem is to raise the value of caring work and to ensure that whoever does it gets more credit and money for it. Otherwise, caring work will be what's left over, the work that's continually passed on down the chain. Sadly, the value ascribed to the labor of raising a child has always been low relative to the value of other kinds of labor, and under the impact of globalization, it has sunk lower still. The low value placed on caring work is due neither to an absence of demand for it (which is always high) nor to the simplicity of the work (successful caregiving is not easy) but rather to the cultural politics underlying this global exchange.

The declining value of child care anywhere in the world can be compared to the declining value of basic food crops relative to manufactured goods on the international market. Though clearly more essential to life, crops such as wheat, rice, or cocoa fetch low and declining prices while the prices of manufactured goods (relative to primary goods) continue to soar in the world market. And just as the low market price of primary produce keeps the third world low in the community of nations, the low market value of care keeps low the status of the women who do it.

One way to solve this problem is to get fathers to contribute more child care. If fathers worldwide shared child care labor more equitably, care would spread laterally instead of being passed down a social-class ladder, diminishing in value along the way. Culturally, Americans have begun to embrace this idea, but they've yet to put it into practice on a truly large scale [see Richard Weissbourd, "Redefining Dad," *TAP*, December 6, 1999]. This is where norms and policies established in the first world can have perhaps the greatest influence on reducing costs along global care chains.

According to the International Labor Organization, half of the world's women between ages 15 and 64 are working in paid jobs. Between 1960 and 1980, 69 out of 88 countries for which data are available showed a growing proportion of women in paid work (and the rate of increase has skyrocketed since the 1950s in the United States, Scandinavia, and the United Kingdom). If we want developed societies with women doctors, political leaders, teachers, bus drivers, and computer programmers, we will need qualified people to help care for children. And there is no reason why every society cannot enjoy such loving paid child care. It may even remain the case that Vicky Diaz is the best person to provide it. But we would be wise to adopt the perspective of the critical modernist and extend our concern to the potential hidden losers in the care chain. These days, the personal is global.

1. Diagram a global care chain as described by Hochschild. Describe the costs and benefits of people at each link in the chain. What things could be described as a deficit or surplus at each link? How do you think the perception of what is lost and gained change based on the perspective of people who represent different links in the chain?

2. Hochschild ends the essay by saying "the personal is global." What else does this apply to in your life? Think about anything from your clothes to your phone, or even your education.

3. Hochschild describes three perspectives of global care chains: the primordialist, the sunshine modernist, and the critical modernist. Which of these perspectives is closest to your own? How do you justify your position? What has led you to adopt this perspective?

Hungry Planet: What the World Eats *is the result of the collaborative efforts of husband-and-wife team* Peter Menzel, photojournalist, *and* Faith D'Aluisio, writer. *Previously a television news producer,* D'Aluisio *has co-authored a number of other works with Menzel, including* Women in the Material World (1996), Man Eating Bugs: the Art and Science of Eating Insects (1998), Robo Sapiens: Evolution of a New Species (2000), *and* What I Eat: Around the World in 80 Diets (2010). Menzel's *photography has appeared in* National Geographic *and* Smithsonian.

HUNGRY PLANET: WHAT THE WORLD EATS

BY FAITH D'ALUISIO AND PETER MENZEL

Peter Menzel and I invited ourselves to dinner with 30 families in 24 countries to explore humankind's oldest social activity, eating. Anyone who remembers grocery shopping 20 years ago knows that the U.S. diet has changed rapidly, but fewer people realize that this transformation is worldwide. Some dietary changes are due to globalization, as largescale capitalism reaches new places. Others are due to rising affluence, as people in formerly impoverished places gain the means to vary their diet—first eating more meat and fish, then pizza and burgers. And some changes are due to the tides of migration, as travelers, immigrants, and refugees bring thier own foods to new lands and acquire new tastes in return. To learn more, we watched typical families the world over as they farmed, shopped, cooked, and ate. At the end of each visit, we created a protrait of the family surrounded by a week's worth of their groceries. The sum, we hope, is a culinary atlas of the planet at a time of extraordinary change.

This book began with a single mouthful of noodles. In the mid-1990's, Peter and I found ourselves in a small covered motorboat off the southeastern coast of the island of New Guinea speeding through the Arafura Sea. It was early spring—typhoon season was approaching. At this time of year, storms can come up so quickly that the local charter planes suspend operations at the slightest hint of bad weather, and even the illegal fishing trawlers plundering the tropical seas around the island are extra careful. Because our assignment schedule was tight, we couldn't wait for a less stormy day. Instead, we hunted for an experienced boat captain willing to make the seven-hour journey to the Asmat— heavily forested section of the Indonesian province of Papua—one of the most remote places on earth.

Peter is a photojournalist and I am a writer, and we have worked together in almost 50 countries over the last 12 years. We generally focus on international stories, and that day eight years ago we were headed to the Asmat to document the lives of its hunting and gathering inhabitants.

From the Asmat's ramshackle capital, Agars, we took a 40-foot longboat three hours up the Pomats River to the village of Sitwa. It was a small, poor place deep in the rain forest, a collection of wooden huts without running water, electricity, telephones, or roads of any kind. Its people live hand to mouth, felling towering sago palm trees and mashing the pulp to make their staple food, a kind of bread. When they can get them, they eat sago grubs. Occasionally, they get fish from the river. It was the steamiest, swampiest place I'd ever been. And it was there, an hour or two after our arrival, that this book began.

Peter and I were (respectively) photographing and talking with a tall skinny man and his two sons, all three of whom showed the marks of hard living. Like many in the village, the man was blind in one eye from vitamin deficiencies: the children had skin diseases and looked seriously undernourished. As we were talking, the older boy pulled a dry brick of instant ramen noodles out of its wrapper and munched it down. His naked, pot-bellied little brother tipped the ramen's flavoring packet into his own mouth and worked the powder around with his tongue until it dissolved. I was mesmerized. I saw this scene play out again and again during our time in Sawa, a place with next to no connection to the rest of the world—children eating an uncooked convenience food intended to simplify the busy lives of people very far away.

I asked a Catholic priest, a longtime resident missionary, about the noodles. He said that logging money had begun to trickle into the villages of these hunters and gatherers. Accompanying the cash came the first merchant to Sawa, a Sulawesian who sold dried food and snacks. Now there's nothing intrinsically wrong with the occasional quick snack of ramen noodles in processed broth, but your don't have to be a food activist to wonder if it is a good idea for the Asmatian, already struggling to find basic nourishment, to dose themselves with jolts of sugar, salt, and artificial flavors.

Since that visit to the Asmat we've seen similar scenes worldwide and have noticed that something odd—even revolutionary—is going on in the world of food. Producing and consuming food is one of humankind's oldest and most basic activities, but the signs of change are everywhere. Riding in taxis through Beijing, we'd see scads of Kentucky Fried Chicken outlets springing up. A grandfather in rural China who remembers the pain of hunger railed against the young Chinese he sees now, wasting food. Here at home, on assignment in the Midwest, we saw endless rows of corn and soy and learned that much of it is now genetically modified. (For better or worse, we Americans don't know when we are eating GM foods—and when we aren't.) In the suburbs of Paris, we met French teenagers whose favorite meals were Pad Thai and sushi. A young mother living in Mexico told me that she had no idea what were the ingredients of soft drinks. Her sedentary family of five was drinking six gallons of Coca-Cola a week, to the exclusion of most other beverages, even as she worried about the family's growing weight and dental problems.

The global marketplace has changed the way people are eating. Societies that are becoming less physically active are also increasing their consumption of energy-dense foods. Even without the academic studies, it's easy to spot—just look around. Many affluent countries are overfed. And unfortunately, it seems that in the developing world, even before people attain a level of influence that helps ensure their adequate nutrition, they are eating in ways almost guaranteed to make them less healthy. As charitable organizations continue their desperately important campaigns against world hunger, others begin equally important campaigns against world obesity. Meanwhile, activists left, right, and center denounce food corporations, food scientists, food conservationists, and food regulators.

To try to make sense of this fascinating, baffling, important muddle, we worked our way around the world and looked at the everyday food of everyday people everywhere—the heaping plates at middle-class mealtimes, the meager communal bowls shared by families crushed by poverty, the sacks of grain served up by overworked aid organizations, the clamorous aisles in hypermarkets, the jam-packed shelves in mom-and-pops, the foods prescribed by religious doctrine, the foods of celebration, subsidized foods. We met people along the way who helped us illustrate the bewildering diversity of what humankind eats in the 21st century: global food, snack food, fast food, junk food, health food, functional food, complimentary food, fortified food, organic food, processed food.

The result—the book in your hands—is not a diet book. Nor is it a jeremiad about supposedly evil corporations, or the supposed enemies of progress, or any of the other sides in the debate about the politics of food. Rather, it is an attempt at a global portrait at a time of momentous change—a freeze-frame snapshot of a fast-moving target.

PROCESS

Gathering information for any project that spans multiple countries is dauntingly difficult, but this one was particularly hard, not least because I often had to introduce concepts that are taken for granted in the developed world. Take, for instance, the idea of a recipe. At Breidjing Refugee Camp in eastern Chad, I asked our translator, Hassane, about the recipe for *aiysh*, the thick porridge that is the staple food of the Sudanese families in the camp. Hassane asked, "There is no such plan for cooking. She learned it from her mother." "I realize that." I replied, "but I must write down how *aiysh* is made, so that the people who read this book can make sense of the food and the process that D'jimia uses to make it." "They only make it, they don't talk about it," he argued. "I realize that, Hassane," I tried again, "but D'jimia will talk about it if we ask her. Please tell her that I have watched many women make *aiysh*, and now I want to ask about the method she uses, so I can write it down for the book."

Peter had exited this conversation, understandably enough, and was photographing at the next tent block, where a group of men were slaughtering a goat for the celebration of the end of Ramadan. D'jimia and the chief of her tent block—who was translating Hassane's Arabic into D'jimia's native Massalit—watched our exchange with interest.

"This is much too difficult," Hassane repeated, shaking his head, as we began anew—from English to Arabic, Arabic to Massalit, and back again. Within a short time, D'jimia had outlined the instructions for making *aiysh*, and we had moved on to talking about the life she and her five children used to lead and the plentiful food they'd had in Sudan, before being forced into Chad by the Janjawiid.

But the flow of information was not just one-way. Sometimes the project taught our subjects as much as it taught us. After our visit to the British village of Collingbourne Ducis in Wiltshire and the subsequent family food portrait, Deb Baintone e-mailed: "I can't believe that I was honest enough to let you photograph the amount of Mars bars I ate in a week—the average British family will be pleased to see that! I eat hardly any these days, so I suppose I've moved on to something equally unhealthy—scary thought, if I've started to get remotely healthy!"

In Shingkhey, a remote hillside village of a dozen homes, Nalim and Namgay's family assembles in the prayer room of their three-story rammed-earth house with one week's worth of food for their extended family of thirteen. Family members: Sangay Kandu, 39, Sangay, 35, holding Tandin Wangchuk (7 months), Sangay Zam (12, daughter of Sangay Kandu and Sangay), Chato Namgay (14, monk, son of Sangay Kandu and Sangay), Chato Geltshin (12, son of Sangay Kandu and Sangay).

The Mustapha family in their courtyard in Dar es Salaam village, Chad, with a week's worth of food. Gathered around Mustapha Abdallah Ishakh, 46 (turban), and Khadidja Baradine, 42 (orange scarf), are Abdel Kerim, 14, Amna, 12 (standing), Nafissa, 6, and Halima, 18 months. Lying on a rug are (left to right) Fatna, 3, granddaughter Amna Ishakh (standing in for Abdallah, 9, who is herding), and Rawda, 5. Cooking method: wood fire. Food preservation: natural drying.

The Madsen family in their living room in Cap Hope village, Greenland, with a week's worth of food. Standing by the TV are Emil Madsen, 40, and Erika Madsen, 26, with their children (left to right) Martin, 9, Belissa, 6, and Abraham, 12. Cooking method: gas stove. Food preservation: refrigerator-freezer. Favorite foods? Emil: polar bear. Erika: narwhal skin. Abraham and Belissa: Greenlandic food. Martin: Danish food.

The Ayme family in their kitchen house in Tingo, Ecuador, a village in the central Andes, with one week's worth of food. Ermelinda Ayme Sichigalo, 37, and Orlando Ayme, 35, sit flanked by their children (left to right): Livia, 15, Natalie, 8, Moises, 11, Alvarito, 4, Jessica, 10, Orlando hijo (Junior, held by Ermelinda), 9 months, and Mauricio, 30 months. Not in photograph: Lucia, 5, who lives with her grandparents to help them out. Cooking method: wood fire.

1. What kind of factors determine the quality and quantities within a family's diet?

2. Think about previous attempts to feed the hungry in other countries. Why do you think that hunger is a persistent problem in the world?

Patrick Symmes is a writer and freelance journalist for magazines including Harper's, Outside, *and* Conde Nast Traveler. *Symmes specializes in issues such as insurgencies, global environmental problems, and the geopolitics involved with each.*

THIRTY DAYS AS A CUBAN

BY PATRICK SYMMES

Pinching pesos and dropping pounds in Havana

In the first two decades of my life I don't believe I ever went more than nine hours without eating. Later on I was subjected to longer bouts—in China in the 1980s, traveling with insurgents in remote areas of Colombia and Nepal, crossing South America by motorcycle, deeply broke—but I always returned home, feasted, ate whatever, whenever, and put back on what weight I'd lost—and more. I'd undergone the usual trajectory of American life, gaining a pound a year, decade after decade. By the time I resolved to go to Cuba, and live for a month on what a Cuban must live on, I was 219 pounds, the most I'd ever weighed in my life.

In Cuba the average salary is $20 a month. Doctors might make $30; many people make only $10. I decided to award myself the salary of a Cuban journalist: $15 a month, the wages of an official intellectual. I'd always wanted to be an intellectual, and $15 was a substantial kick above the proles building brick walls or cutting cane for $12, and almost twice the $8 paid to many retirees. With this money I would have to buy my basic ration of rice, beans, potatoes, cooking oil, eggs, sugar, coffee, and anything else I needed.

I knew it would be hard to give up food, and so I began my Cuban diet while still in New York City, shaking off nine pounds in the two months before my departure. Time and again, as I prepared for this trip, horrified friends speculated on what food I was gorging on, what special items I was rushing to consume. Their operating assumption was that being deprived of some cherished item for thirty days was an unbearable test. They were worried about ice cream. In my experience, no one who is hungry craves ice cream.

A monthly oil ration, photograph by Patrick Symmes; A shop on Calle Industria, photograph © Lorenzo Castore/Agence VU/Aurora Photos; A standard ration board, photograph by Patrick Symmes

My first half hour inside Cuba was spent at the metal detectors. Then, as part of a new regimen, unknown in my previous fifteen years coming here, I was given an intense but amateurish interrogation. This had nothing to do with me: all foreigners on the small turboprop from the Bahamas were separated out and questioned at length. The Cuban government was nervous about solitary foreign travelers because Human Rights Watch had recently been through, on tourist visas, and a State Department contractor, also traveling on a tourist visa, had been caught distributing USB drives and satphones to opposition figures. Tourists were dangerous.

As in Israel, an agent in plain clothes asked me detail-oriented questions of no importance ("What town are you going to? Where is that?"), designed to provoke me, reveal some inconsistency, or show nervousness. He didn't look in my wallet and ask why, if I was staying in Cuba for a month, I had less than twenty dollars. The supervisor's gaze settled on the other passengers. Passed. "Thirty days," I told the lady who stamped my tourist visa. The maximum.

There was a sign hanging from the airport ceiling with a drawing of a bus on it. But there was no bus. Not now, a woman at the information desk explained. There would be a bus—one—tonight, around 8 p.m., to take the airport workers home.

That was six hours from now. Central Havana was ten miles away. Since taxis cost about $25—more than my total budget for the next month—I was going to have to walk.

A daily bread ration, photograph © Alfredo Falvo/Contrasto/Redux; An agro, photograph by Patrick Symmes; The meat annex of an agro, photograph by Patrick Symmes

The same woman pulled from her uniform pocket a couple of aluminum coins, which she gave to me: 40 centavos, or about 2 U.S. cents. Out on the highway, a few miles from here, I might find a city bus. And in Havana I might find, must find, a way to survive for a month. I had to shoulder my knapsack and start walking, the aluminum coins clicking in my pocket. I strolled out of the terminal, across the parking lot, out the driveway, and turned down the only road, putting the outside world behind me with a steady slog. Every few minutes a taxi would pull up, beeping, or a private car would stop, offering to take me for half the official price. I walked on, slowly, past the old terminals, along scrubby fields. Billboards trumpeted old messages: *Bush Terrorist.* After forty minutes I passed over a railroad crossing, came out to the highway, and got lucky. The bus for Havana was right there. An hour later I was in central Havana and on foot, searching for an old friend.

The first people I spoke to in the city—total strangers who lived near my friend[1]—brought up the ration system. With no prompting from me, they pulled out their ration book and bitched.

The book—called the *libreta*—is the foundational document of Cuban life. Nothing important about the ration system has changed: although it is now printed in a vertical format, the book looks identical to the one issued annually for decades.

What has changed is the ink: there is less written in the book. There are fewer entries, for smaller amounts, than even in 1995, during the starving time of the "Special Period." In the intervening years, the Cuban economy has recovered; the Cuban ration system has not. In 1999, a Cuban development minister told me that the monthly ration supplied enough food to last just nineteen days, but predicted that the amount would soon climb. It has declined. Although the total amount of food available in Cuba is greater, and caloric consumption is up, that is no thanks to the ration system. The growth has occurred in privatized markets and cooperative gardens and through massive imports, while state food production fell 13 percent last year and the ration shrank with it. It is commonly agreed that a monthly food ration now contains just twelve days of food. I was here to make my own calculation: how could anyone survive the month on twelve days of food?

There is one ration book per family. Goods are distributed at a series of neighborhood bodegas (one for dairy and eggs; another for "protein"; another for bread; the largest for dry goods and everything from coffee to cooking oil to cigarettes). Each store has a clerk who writes in the amount issued to the family. My friend's neighbors—husband, wife, and grandson—had received a standard ration of staples, which was, per person:

> 4 pounds refined sugar
>
> 1 pound crude sugar
>
> 1 pound grain
>
> 1 piece fish
>
> 3 rolls

They laughed when I asked if there was beef.

"Chicken," the wife said, but this produced howls of protest. "When was there chicken?" her husband asked. "Well, that's true," she said. "It has been a few months." The "protein" ration was delivered every fifteen days and was ground mystery meat, mixed with a large amount of soy paste (if the meat was pork, this was falsely called *picadillo*;

if it was chicken, it was called *pollo con suerte*, or chicken and luck). Usually there was enough for about four hamburgers a month, but so far in January they had received only one fish each—usually a dried, oily mackerel.

And there were eggs. The most reliable of all protein sources, these were called *salvavidas*, or lifesavers. There used to be an egg a day; then it became an egg every other day; now it was an egg every third day. I would have ten for the next month.

The husband spent a full quarter of his tiny salary on the electric bill. The family survived only because, in his job as a state chauffeur, he could steal about five liters of gasoline every week.

A daily bread ration, photograph © Alfredo Falvo/Contrasto/Redux; An agro, photograph by Patrick Symmes; The meat annex of an agro, photograph by Patrick Symmes

Eventually my friend appeared and squired me off to a private home in the Plaza neighborhood, where I had arranged to rent an apartment for the month—the one expense left out of my accounting here. It was spartan, in the Cuban style: two rooms, cushionless chairs, a double burner on a countertop, and a half-size refrigerator. I unloaded my pockets, stashing away the food I had bought in the Bahamian airport: some bagels, a can of fruit punch, sandwiches, and—my emergency stash—a packet of sesame sticks from the airplane. With a fourteen-hour trip from New York behind me, I ate one of the sandwiches and went to sleep.

On my second day, I gnawed on a sesame bagel, absentmindedly consuming the whole thing, as if there would always be another. According to a calorie-counting application on my cell phone, the bagel had 440 calories. Everything I ate for the next month would be entered on that little keypad, recorded, summed up by day and week, divided into protein, carbohydrates, and fat, graphed in scrolling bars. An active man of my size (six foot two, 210 pounds) needs about 2,800 calories a day to maintain his weight. I had no other food supplies yet, and I finished breakfast when the housekeeper working for my landlord gave me two thimbles of coffee, larded with sugar (75 calories).

Just as Cubans exploit loopholes to survive, I worked my obvious foreignness to my benefit, wandering that day in and out of fancy hotels few Cubans could enter. This gave me access to air-conditioning, toilet paper, and music. I blew past security at the Habana Libre, the old Hilton, and rode the elevator to the top floor, which offered commanding views of Havana at dusk. The nightclub wasn't open yet, but I barged in anyway, discovering a rehearsal in progress. A Russian rocker, backed by more than thirty musicians, was working through his set in preparation for some later gig. They had been issued bottled water and tea, which I consumed in large amounts. Tea's astringent taste—mediated by lots of sugar—finally made sense to me. This was the drink of the novice monk, the cold and hungry. It was an appetite killer.

There had been catering. Only one and a half cheese sandwiches remained, abandoned on a napkin near the string section; during a crescendo I stuffed them into my pockets. I walked the hour back across Havana to my room, passing dozens of new stores, butcher shops, bars, cafeterias and cafés, pizza joints, and other prolific suppliers of hard-currency food. I lingered, looking at the immense frozen turkey breasts for sale in a shop window.

By the time I got to my room, the sandwiches had disintegrated in my pockets, a mass of crumbs, butter, and cheese product, but I ate them, slowly, dragging the experience out. I'd always scorned the Cubans who cheered the regime for a sandwich, but by day two I was ready to denounce Obama for a cookie.

On the morning of the third day I walked for more than two hours through Havana in search of food, burning 600 calories, the equivalent of those cheese sandwiches. I had wrongly assumed that I could simply buy the food I needed for the month. But as an American I was ineligible for the ration, through which rice costs a penny a pound. As a "Cuban" living on $15 a month I could not afford to buy food outside the system, in the expensive dollar stores. Cubans called these small stores, which sold everything from batteries and beef to cooking oil and diapers, *el shopping*. After hours of frustration, unable to buy any food at all, I rode the bus back to my apartment.

I had no lunch. I tried reading, but I had brought only books about hardship and suffering, like *Les Misérables*. I started with an easier, more comic take on loneliness and deprivation, *Sailing Alone Around the World* by Joshua Slocum, and consumed 146 pages on my first day. Slocum got across the Atlantic on little more than biscuits, coffee, and flying fish, and I took particular satisfaction when, mid-Pacific, he discovered that his potatoes were ridden with moths and was forced to chuck the valuable rations overboard. But then he would do something unconscionable, like cook an Irish stew or call on some reserve of smoked venison from Tierra del Fuego. A passing boat even tossed him a bottle of Spanish wine once, the bastard. Reading at this rate, books were another thing I would run out of.

Finally, unable to lie still any longer, I raced out of the house and, following a tip, found a house a few blocks away with a cardboard sign on the gate reading cafe. Behind the house there was a barred window, and I put the equivalent of 40 cents through the bars. A woman passed out a roll filled with processed lunch meat. For another 12 cents I got a small glass of papaya juice. Although I tried to eat slowly, lunch vanished within moments. At this rate—half a dollar a meal—my entire cash supply would be eaten up, and I left her back yard vowing to eat almost nothing for dinner.

Worse news awaited me in the morning when, upon dressing, I discovered that the zipper on my pants was broken. In another effort to look and feel Cuban, I had brought only two pairs of pants. Pants are one of the many non-food items distributed by ration, and that meant, typically, one pair a year. Most Cubans got along with just a couple of items of clothing of each type. So the broken zipper would have to be repaired—there were no pants in January. A few feeble attempts to repair it myself failed. I was going to have to spend some money, or trade something, for a tailor's work. Breakfast: coffee, two cups, with sugar. 75 calories total.

I went food shopping on day four, a ludicrous experience. By chance I had ended up taking an apartment near the largest and best market in Havana, which was neither large nor good. The market was an *agro*, meaning a place for farm produce. These are sometimes referred to as farmers' markets, but there was no farmer meets-consumer bonhomie, only a roaring, crowded, sweaty pen of stalls selling the same narrow band of goods at prices set by the state: pineapples, eggplants, carrots, green peppers, tomatoes, onions, yucca, garlic, plantains, and not much else. There was a separate room specializing in pork, with quivering heaps of dull pink meat turned over by bare-handed men and measured out by dull knives. Meat was beyond my reach, though "fat" was listed at only 13 pesos (or 49 cents) a pound.

I waited in line to change my entire stock of money—eighteen hard currency *pesos convertibles*—into the regular Cuban pesos.[2] The resulting pile of worn, dirty bills added up to 400 pesos, worth about $16 at the Havana street rate. Then I fought through the crowds to buy one eggplant (10 pesos), four tomatoes (15), garlic (2), and a small bunch of carrots (13). At a bakery counter a woman selling bread rolls affirmed they were only for people with ration books—but then threw me five rolls and greedily snatched 5 pesos out of my hand. The only love came from the tomato vendor, who threw in an extra nightshade.

I bought three pounds of rice for a little more than a dime, and some red beans, spending a catastrophic $2 for what would, in the end, produce only a handful of meals.

Young hustlers followed me to the exit muttering, "Shrimp, Shrimp, Shrimp." Outside, a man saw me coming and climbed into a tree, descending again with five limes, which he offered me (it was not a lime tree but a drop zone for his black-market produce). I staggered home under the weight of the rice and vegetables, looking, as my landlady later observed, like a divorced man starting his new life.

The accumulated calories inevitably led me to speculate on the other side of things: money. How would I survive a couple of weeks from now, if I was spending the equivalent of $2 at a pop? I continued to hoof it everywhere, taking the hour-long walk just to wander through the tourist hotels of Vedado (without ever spotting another stray sandwich), or stand with my face pressed to the iron grille of some restaurant, watching, with four or five Cubans, the band play a mambo for foreigners.

Every day I was approached by Cubans who said, in one phrase or another, *Give me money.* My own options would be grim in the weeks ahead. Should I stand on the street corner, demanding dollars from strangers? How hungry did you have to get before you became like the teenage girl I overtook on a Vedado sidewalk that afternoon, who, holding a baby on her hip, turned to me and said, *Deseas una chica sucky sucky?*

If I was going to suck something, I knew what it would be. I found myself watching the Ladas as they rolled past, trying to see how many had locking gas caps. With some tubing and a jug, I could get five liters of gasoline and sell it through a friend in Chinatown. But all the cars in Cuba had locking gas caps or were themselves locked behind gates at night. Too many men, harder than I, were already working that line. This was no island for amateur thieves.

I needed coffee, but all stores were barren of this staple. Even the hard-currency shopping in the neighborhood carried no coffee, and repeated tours of the dollar supermarkets in Vedado and at various hotels had revealed no coffee all month. I had once seen a pound of Cubacafe, the dark, export-grade stuff, for sale at a movie theater in Old Havana. But it was 64 pesos, and even while jonesing I could not pay that much or walk that far. From the window of my bathroom I could see that the ration store was open, and so I wandered over.

There were five satchels of coffee on the shelf. It was the light-brown domestic brand, Hola, which sells for a little more than a peso for the first four-ounce bag, and 5 pesos a sack after that. A dozen people were jostling for bread and rice, so I had time to study the two chalkboards listing which goods were available. The larger board listed basic ration goods. Your first four pounds of rice cost 25 centavos; the next pound was 90 centavos. No more than six pounds of rice were allowed in a month, to prevent overselling for profit. The smaller chalkboard listed "liberated products," a briefer list of cigarettes and other items that could be bought without limit.

I called out *El último*, and was now holding a place in line behind the previous last customer. Pretty soon a woman with a plastic bag arrived, cried *El último*, and I lifted a finger. Now she was last. I was served by a smiling but agitated man. He was tall, black, with a scruffy partial beard. He waved his hand when I asked for coffee. No words were necessary: a foreigner cannot buy on the ration, and there was no coffee anyway. I played for time, holding up my end of a conversation in which he was silent but for gestures. No coffee anywhere? I've been all over the city looking for coffee. Nobody has any. I really like coffee. You know what I mean? "Cubans drink a lot of coffee," he finally said. Our bond established, I wiggled my head back and forth and asked, Wasn't there somewhere to get coffee? "No," he said. Really? Maybe someone had some? A little bit? He wiggled his head. The *maybe* gesture.

Who?

"Mrs. ——," he said.

Where was that?

As though guiding a blind man, he came out from behind the counter, took my arm, and led me out onto the street. We went only ten steps down the sidewalk. He turned into the first doorway and absentmindedly grabbed the ass of a passing woman. ("Hey!" she cried, furious. "Who's that?") We stopped at an apartment located directly behind the ration store. He knocked. A woman with a baby answered.

"Coffee," he said.

I produced a 20-peso bill. She handed me one satchel of the Hola and 5 pesos back.

"That's all?" It was three times the price listed at the counter a few steps away, but I found later that Cubans also paid this markup.

He nodded. His name was Jesús.

We went back to the store. "Bread?" I asked. He consulted with his supervisor, who gave a "No" loud enough for the whole store to hear.

I asked again. He asked his boss again. No *no* this time. I handed over the 5-peso note and got five rolls.

From then on, I could buy whatever I wanted. With Jesús on my side, no questions were asked. I never needed a ration book for the common staples, and for the rest of the month I paid the same price as Cubans for the same shit food.

On the sixth day I walked to the suburbs, strolling out of my neighborhood, Plaza, through Vedado and to the west, past the immense *Colón* cemetery, home to the mausoleums and soaring angels of Cuba's once-rich families, as well as the concrete sepulchers of her middle class. A young man named Andy fell into step with me for a while, excited to hear about America ("We all want to go there") and inviting me to a barbershop owned by his friend. Alone again, I passed the occasional café, studying each of these tiny stands. One offered "bread with hamburger" for 10 pesos, the lowest price I had seen yet. But that was still too much for today.

I joined the world of the long-range pedestrian, working my way down a dozen avenues and more than twenty streets in the course of an hour and finding a small bridge over the *Almendares* River that separates Havana proper from Havana greater. Exiles wax nostalgic about the *Almendares*, whose twisting route is overgrown with vines and immense trees, but I always found it depressing or even frightening: a humid, muddy border between the gritty city and the expansive (and expensive) houses of the western suburbs. From a low Oceanside bridge I could see what remained of the sailor scene: a dozen sunken hulls, a few collapsing houseboats, and abandoned boat shacks. Only two boats were in motion: a police launch and a dismasted micro-yacht of twenty feet or so, apparently incapable of reaching Florida.

I made a right turn into Miramar, passing some of Cuba's grandest mansions and many embassies. This was "the zone of the moneybags, foreign firms, and people with lineage," a prostitute says in the book *Havana Babylon*. "Living in Miramar, even in a toilet, is a sign of distinction."

I was pursued by two women waving a gigantic can of tomato sauce and shouting "Fifteen pesos! It's for our children!" I went on but later realized I had made a mistake. At 15 pesos for a restaurant-size container, the tomato sauce had been good value. Stolen food was the cheapest food. And nothing could be more normal here than wandering around with a huge can of something.

A few blocks later I stumbled on the Museum of the Interior Ministry. The museum was staffed by women in khaki MININT uniforms, with green shoulder boards and knee-length skirts. The entrance fee was 2 CUC, they told me. I couldn't pay that, of course. How much was it for a Cuban, I asked? Wrong question. You don't bargain with MININT.

I said I would come back another time, but dawdled in the entrance hall, which had its own exhibits: racks of machine guns, photos of the big MININT headquarters near my apartment, and oversized quotes from Raúl Castro and other officials praising the patriots at MININT for protecting the nation.

One of the women, hair in a tight bun, watched me. Although I took no notes or pictures, she was shrewd.

"Who are you?" she asked.

I smiled and turned to leave.

"Are you a journalist?" she demanded.

"Tourist," I said, over my shoulder, and racewalked away.

"Are you accredited here?" she called after me.

I continued westward on foot for another half hour. I was coated in sweat by the time I reached the house of Elizardo Sánchez, one of MININT's targets.

When I told Sánchez I had walked here, as part of spending thirty days living and eating as a Cuban, he showed me his *libreta*. "They call this the supply booklet, but it's a rationing system, the longest-running one in the world. The Soviets didn't have rationing for as long as Cuba. Even the Chinese didn't ration this long." Shortages began soon after the revolution; a system for the controlled distribution of basic goods was in place by 1962.

After fifty years of progress, the country was effectively bankrupt. In 2009, peas and potatoes had been removed from the ration, and cheap workplace lunches had been shrunk down to snack-size portions. "There was talk of removing things from the ration, or getting rid of it entirely," Sánchez told me, repeating the rumor that captivated all Cubans. But the talk had died on January 1, 2010, when the new *libretas* were handed out, like always.

Sánchez was happily ignorant of the domestic arts. "Four pounds of rice at 25 centavos," he said, trying to recall his monthly allotment. "I think. And, uh, a fifth pound at 90 centavos, I think. Let's consult the women. They dominate on this matter." He called to his common-law wife, Barbara. Aside from being a lawyer who worked on prisoners' cases, she cooked and was helping her mother and another woman run a bakery out of the kitchen. They had bought a bag of flour "on the left," meaning it was stolen or bought from a connection. This cost 30 pesos. With this and some ground beef purchased under the counter at the butchers, they made tiny empanadas that they sold for 3 pesos apiece, or about eight for a dollar. This was how Cuba got along: the ration stores were staffed by neighbors, who stole and resold ingredients, which were then reworked into finished products and sold back to these same neighbors. Eight empanadas would make a lunch, but a dollar was inconceivably beyond my budget. Barbara gave me two, each of which I demolished in a bite.

She listened blankly as I explained my attempt to live on the ration. "It's a great diet plan," she said. Another dissident visiting the house, Richard Rosello, piped in. He'd been filling a notebook with the prices of goods on the parallel markets, also called the clandestine or black-bag markets. "One problem is food," Richard said, "but another is how do you pay your light bill, the gas, the rent? Electricity has gone up four to seven times in cost compared with before." Elizardo was paying nearly 150 pesos a month for electricity—a quarter of the typical salary.

How to get by, then? "Cubans invent something," Barbara said. One trick was "overselling" your cheap, rationed goods at market prices. I'd finally scored my allotment of ten eggs this way. Without a ration book I could not buy the eggs legally. But at dusk the night before, I had waited near my local egg shop and made eyes at an elderly woman who'd emerged with thirty eggs—a month's supply for three people. She'd bought them for 1.5 pesos each and sold me ten of them for 2 pesos apiece. She immediately spent the money on more, turning a profit of three eggs and change. We both walked home gingerly, afraid of smashing a month's protein with a single misstep.

Barbara now pointed out a terrible mistake in my plan. In recent years, most sources outside Cuba reported that the ration includes five pounds of black beans. But it had been years since this was true. This month, the allotment was just eight ounces.

Ten thousand calories had just evaporated from my month.

To make up for this blow, Barbara decided to treat me to a "typical" Cuban lunch. This began with rice, at four or five dry pounds per person each month the mainstay of Cuba's diet. Each citizen could eat about as much cooked rice per day as fits in a condensed-milk can. It was low-quality Vietnamese rice and variously called "creole," "ugly," or "microjet" rice, the last a mocking reference to one of Fidel's plans to boost agricultural production with drip irrigators. A typical lunch included half a can of cooked rice (the other half saved for dinner); it was a gooey mash, but it tasted good enough, sauced by my hunger.

Next was a bowl of bean soup. It had only a handful of beans, but the broth was rich, flavored with beef bones. ("Ten pesos a pound for bones," Barbara noted. "Many people can't afford it.")

I hadn't tasted meat in six days.

Then she gave me half a small sweet potato. "Much better nutritionally than potato!" Elizardo called from somewhere down the hall.

There was also a fried egg, although, as Elizardo noted with another shout, "Eat that egg today and you won't eat one tomorrow." Or the day after.

The egg was wonderful. With my shrunken stomach, the whole meal, including the two little empanadas, was perfectly adequate. I chewed on the bones, extracting small bits of meat. This was the best I'd eaten in days. Barbara carefully preserved the oil from the frying pan.

Richard, with his little notebook of prices, pointed out the math of eating this way. A "monthly basket" of rationed food (which actually lasted just twelve days) cost 12 pesos a person, by government calculation. For the next ten days, people had to buy the same food for about 220 pesos on the various free, parallel, and black markets. That still got you only to day twenty two. A month would run about 450 pesos—more than the entire incomes of millions of Cubans, and that didn't account for clothes, transport, or household goods.

No one could afford cups and plates anymore. These were stolen from state enterprises when possible and traded on the black market. Clothes had to be bought used, at swap meets called *troppings*, a play on the hard-currency *shoppings*. Those who ran out of food went rummaging in dumpsters, or became alcoholics to numb the pain, he said.

Elizardo came back in. "This isn't Haiti, or Sudan," he said. "People aren't falling over in the streets, dead of hunger. Why? Because the government guarantees four or five pounds of sugar, which is high in calories, and bread every day, and enough rice. The problem in Cuba isn't food, or clothes. It's the total lack of civil liberty, and therefore of economic liberty, which is why you have to have the *libreta* in the first place."

As in the rest of the world, the problem of food is really one of access, of money. And the problem of money is one of politics.

On the seventh day I rested. Lying in bed with Victor Hugo, lost in the test of man's goodness, I could forget for an hour at a time that my gums ached, that saliva was bathing my throat.

Havana was changing, as cities do. The historic zone had been placed under the control of Eusebio Leal Spengler, the city historian. Leal had been given special priority for building supplies, labor, trucks, tools, fuel, pipes, cement, wood, even faucets and toilets. But this was not why the people loved him. Instead, my friend explained, the "privileged" access to supplies simply meant that *there was more to steal*.

A friend of mine was renovating in hopes of renting rooms to foreigners, and indeed within a few minutes there was a screech of truck brakes and a great horn blast. Her husband signaled to me urgently, and we threw open the front door. A flatbed truck was waiting. In sixty seconds, three of us unloaded 540 pounds of Portland cement bags. The husband passed some wadded bills to the trucker, who promptly roared off. They had made money off cement destined for some construction job. We spent half an hour moving the bags to a dark corner in a back room, covering them with a tarp because they were printed with blue ink, marking them as state property. Green printing was for school construction. Only cement in red-printed bags could be bought by citizens, in state stores, at $6 a bag.

Unlike most Cuban functionaries, Leal had actually made a difference in people's lives. He rebuilt the old hotels; my friends took 540 pounds of cement for their new tourist bungalow. He restored a museum; they looted tin sheeting for roofs. He sent trucks of lumber into the neighborhood; they made half the wood vanish.

The State owned all. The people appropriated all. A ration system in reverse.

Helping to steal the cement was my first great success. For half an hour of labor, I was paid with a heaping plate of rice and red beans, topped with a banana and a small portion of picadillo. At least 800 calories.

The second week was easier, my two little shelves well stocked with bags of rice and beans, some sweet potatoes at 80 centavos a pound, and my bottle of smuggled whiskey still half full. I had nine, and then eight, and then seven eggs, though the refrigerator was otherwise barren.

I had given up luxuries like sandwiches (or sandwich, singular: I had bought only one, but the expense still haunted me). On day ten I found I had 100 pesos left. As with the eggs, could imagine a careful, slow reduction over the next twenty days, but my budget and diet could be equally ruined by a slip that left a yolk on the floor. It all came down to a question of how long the rice would last: with just 5 pesos per day remaining, I could afford no major purchases for the rest of my stay. I learned to suppress my appetite, walking past the queues of Cubans buying tiny balls of fried dough for a peso apiece. My only indulgence was a bar of stiff peanut butter, handmade by farmers, which sold for 5 pesos in the *agros*. With restraint, this little slab of about six tablespoons of crudely ground, heavily sweetened peanut could be made to last two days. The poorest *campesinos* could be seen nibbling on these packets of peanut butter, carefully rewrapping after each bite.

Another thing I had in common with most Cubans was that I did absolutely no work during my thirty days. That is to say, I worked hard and often at my own projects—I hauled cement and shoveled gravel for food, and wrote a lot—but it was not state labor, not the kind of work that is counted in the columns of official Cuba, where more than 90 percent of people are state employees. Why should I get a job? Nobody else took theirs seriously, and the oldest joke in Havana is still the best: They pretend to pay us, we pretend to work.[3]

So I had time on my hands. That night I heard music and found a series of stages set up along 23rd Street, culminating in a good rock band playing under a rising moon. I sat on the pedestal of some heroic obscurity—the statue of a mother thrusting her son toward battle. After a while a small girl, seven or eight, came and sat on the stone.

"*Caramelo?*" she said. Sweet?

"I don't have any."

"None?"

"No."

"Not one?"

"No."

Then the usuals: where are you from, where do you live, why are you here? And again: "Some money?"

"I don't have any."

"But foreigners always have so much money."

"Yes, in my country I have money. But here, I live like a Cuban."

"Give me a peso?"

I can't. I'm playing a game, my dear. I'm pretending to be broke. I'm living like your parents for a while. I haven't eaten in nine hours. In the past eleven days I've missed 12,000 calories off my normal diet. My teeth hurt so badly.

Or, in Spanish, "*No.*"

I finally strode home to a long-awaited celebration. It was Friday, and tonight was the weekly Eating of the Meat. Although the day had so far been one of my worst—less than 1,000 calories by 9 p.m., with a huge amount of walking—I was determined to make up for it with a feast. I prepared rice, put a single sweet potato in the pressure cooker—known to Cubans as The-One-Fidel-Gave-Us, because they were handed out in an energy-saving scheme—and poured a precious glass of whiskey (250 calories) on the rocks, all with a side of yesterday's beans and rice. Of necessity the portions were small.

From the freezer I drew my protein, one of four breaded chicken cutlets for the month. I fired the stove carelessly and burned the cutlet black, though at the table it proved cold and soggy on the inside. It was not chicken. It was not even the "formed chicken" it claimed to be. The principal ingredients were listed as wheat paste and soy. Close inspection revealed no chicken at all. I was eating a breaded sponge with only 180 calories. Ah, for a McNugget.

In the end, I crossed the 2,000- calorie barrier for the first time in ten days, just barely. Discounting for a huge amount of walking and a little dancing, this left me at my familiar benchmark of 1,700 calories. But my stomach was full when I went to bed.

Or so I thought. After two hours of sleep, I woke with insomnia, the companion to hunger. From 1 a.m. until dawn I lay in bed, five hours of swatting at mosquitoes, tossing, reading Victor Hugo and Alexandre Dumas *père*.

Still, I can't compare my situation to real hunger. As Hugo notes, "Behind living on a little lies the art of living on nothing." I sank into thousands of pages of nineteenth-century France, two authors describing revolution, forced marches, and real starvation. "When one has not eaten," Hugo writes, "it is very queer. . . . He chewed that inexpressible thing which is called the cud of bitterness. A horrible thing, which includes days without bread, nights without sleep." So came the dawn, my twelfth.

Suddenly, fortune and happiness. The next night, as I sat in front of my apartment watching the street, my neighbor came walking down the alley holding a phone. A phone call. For me. It was a friend of a friend, visiting Cuba with her boyfriend. They were verifiable ain't-we-grand Americans, and I instantly smelled free food. They'd landed in Havana and, unfamiliar with the city or Spanish, were inviting me to dine with them. We went for a walk around Vedado and I carefully avoided pleading for food, playing the stoic. They bought dinner at a tourist restaurant, and for the first time I ate pork. The next afternoon we met again. I took them to see a Santería initiation, an hour of steamy drumming in a tiny apartment, complete with three separate acts of possession. Another invitation to dine at a fancy restaurant followed.

More pork!

Cubans marinate *lechón*, the innocent little suckling pig, with garlic and bitter orange, and slow-cook it until you can eat it with a spoon. Along with the glistening fat and protein, we were served a platter of rice and beans, exactly what I ate twice a day in my own kitchen. The platter would make four meals for me, I explained.

"Excuse me," the boyfriend said, helping himself. "I'm just going to eat your Thursday."

Like the hundreds of Cubans whom I have fed over the years, I sang for my supper. The lore of Afro-Cuban cults. The history of buildings I had never seen before. Strolls in the shoes of Capone, Lansky, Churchill, and Hemingway. Socialism jokes. The arts of the ration. The secret of the daiquiri. Both of those nights I had some pork, rice and beans, and a pair of cocktails.

Despite the meat I was hardly better off—just 2,100 calories each day, compared with my usual 1,700. But the meals added to my psychological well-being. I had carried off a respite, a vacation, from the grinding anxiety of seeing my dry goods evaporate.

The next morning I found a woman riffling through my garbage. She wanted glass bottles or anything valuable: I gave her my broken pants. She was eighty-four years old, the same age as my mother, and lived on a pension of 212 pesos a month, or a little over $8. She scavenged in the trash for items—to the fury of my housekeeper, who considered the trash her own resource—and worked as a *colero*, or professional line-waiter, for five families on this block. She took their ration books to the bodega, collected and delivered the monthly goods, and was paid a total of about 133 pesos for this. She was sucking on an asthma inhaler that cost 20 pesos, or about 75 cents, but only the first one came at that price: others had to be bought on the black market at several dollars apiece.

In return for my pants, she mentioned that the "free" bakery was stocked. This was the non-ration bakery, where anyone could buy a loaf. The price is four times that of the ratio bakeries, but there is much more bread. I retrieved a plastic bag, walked eight blocks (passing three empty ration bakeries), and bought a loaf for 10 pesos.

 As I walked home, a woman passing the other way asked, "They have bread?" She doubled her pace.

Then, as I passed a chess game under a shortleaf fig tree, a man looked up and asked the same.

"Yes, there is bread," I told him.

He toppled the pieces, rolled up the board, and both players decamped for the bakery.

Breakfast had been a tiny, hard plantain, bought from a man in an alley. With coffee and sugar, it was less than 200 calories. Lunch was an egg and two slivers of the new bread, for another 380.

There were three dollars in my wallet and seventeen days to go.

A catastrophic mistake. I had been afoot all afternoon, my blood sugar bottoming out, and when I passed an alley with a small piece of cardboard reading pizza, I stopped and bought one. The basic pizza—a six-inch disk of dough smeared with ketchup and a tablespoon of cheese—cost 10 pesos. But I impulsively supersized my order, adding chorizo. It was now a 15-peso snack.

In my apartment I set the little pizza down and stared in horror. 15 pesos was an incredible, budget-busting 60 cents. I could have bought pounds of rice for that amount. Staring at the puny thing, smaller than a single slice in America, I began trembling. I had to sit down. Then I burst into tears. For a good ten minutes I wept, cursing myself. Moron! Fool! Idiot!

I had spent a fifth of my remaining money on impulse. Now I had just 64 pesos to survive the next seventeen days. What would happen to me now? How would I eat when I ran out of beans, which were already low? What if there was another mistake? What if I was robbed? How would I get to the airport on the last day if I didn't have even a few pennies for bus fare?

Crying releases not just tension and fear but endorphins. Around the time the pizza had cooled down, I had, too. I ate it carefully, with a knife and fork, and a glass of ice water. This "meal" lasted less than two minutes. It was the low point of my month. An hour later, there was a knock on the door. The child of one of my neighbors was outside. "*Patri!*" she cried. "*Patri!*"

I went out. She handed me a shoe box. It was heavy and covered in packing tape. Someone had stopped by—another American visiting Cuba—and dropped it off. In the kitchen I cut it open and found a note from my wife and young son, and three dozen homemade tea cookies.

I ate ten cookies. Ambush to escape. Tears to peace. Damnation to joy.

I rationed the rest of the cookies: five per day until they ran low, then two per day, and finally I disassembled the box with a knife and ate the crumbs out of the corners.

Once a day I indulged my vanity, standing shirtless in front of a mirror and staring at a man I had not seen in fifteen years. I had lost four, then six, then eight pounds. But the stomach and mind adjust with frightening ease. My first week had been pained and starving. The second was pained and hungry. Now, in my third week, I was eating less than ever but was at ease both physically and mentally.

I had my worst day so far, eating just 1,200 calories. That was the intake of an American POW in Japan during WWII.

I went back to my friends the cement thieves, and after much waiting, the woman cooked me a generous dinner, cackling with laughter over "your experiment." She had fried (in oil stolen from a school) some ground chicken (bought from a friend who stole it), which she served with the "ugly" rice from the ration and a single tiny beet. After the meal, she even made me some eggnog, but in a Cuban serving—one mouthful, in an espresso cup. There were also a few spoonfuls of papaya (1 peso each, at a cheap market she recommended), cooked down in sugar syrup.

"It's impossible," she said of my attempt to be officially Cuban. For survival, everyone had to have "an extra," some income outside the system. Her husband rented a room to a Norwegian sex tourist. Her neighbor sold lunches to the workers who'd recently lost their canteen meals. Her own mother wandered the streets with pitchers of coffee and a cup, selling jolts of caffeine. Her friend around the corner stole the cooking oil and resold it for 20 pesos a pint. Another neighbor stole the ground chicken and resold it for 15 pesos a pound. ("Good quality, a very good price, you should get some," and I did.)

Her meal was the only one I ate that day, the calories undercut by an astonishing walk not just across Havana but completely around it, passing in a giant loop down the carbuncled streets, through big hotels, past dim houses, among people sleeping without roofs, sitting on packing crates, onward all the time, hours in rotation through noon, afternoon, evening, on wide avenues and in narrow alleys, across Plaza, Vedado, Centro, Old Havana, into Cerro, out through Plaza again, into Vedado again, two, four, six, eight miles, past the bus station, the sports stadium, burning holes in my shoes, and then to bed.

My feet hurt. But there wasn't the slightest complaint from my stomach.

I used to say that 10 percent of everything was stolen in Cuba, to be resold or repurposed. Now I think the real figure is 50 percent. Crime is the system. On the sidewalk in front of my ration store one day, I saw a teenager with a punk-rock haircut, idling in his shiny Mitsubishi Lancer and playing with what I mistook for an iPhone. "It's not an iPhone," he corrected me. "It's an iTouch."

These sell for $200, or 5,300 pesos. Some people have money, even here. The only certainty is that they didn't make that money in any legitimate way.

I walked to the sweeping Riviera, where the gaming floor was cleared by nationalization just a year after it opened. (Meyer Lansky, the owner, famously said he had "crapped out.") In the gym I weighed myself: 200 pounds. In 18 days I'd lost ten pounds, a rate that would result in hospitalization in the United States.

On the way home, a woman asked me where the P2 bus was found. I mangled the answer. "Oh, I thought you were a Cuban," she said.

Lose weight, change nationalities. I laughed off her mistake and went on, but a minute later she was chasing me down.

"Hey, invite me to lunch," she said. "Anyplace." I shook my head, no.

"Lunch," she called after me. "Dinner. As you like."

At home, I opened the fridge and counted: five eggs left.

Like the woman looking for the P2, I'd become direct. I walked two miles out to Cerro, a bad neighborhood. This took me right through an alley lined with rusting wrecks of trucks, past a crumbling sports stadium, through an overgrown park and a grove of trees, to the front door of the Ministry of the Interior. This is the famous building with a giant Che Guevara on it. It was guarded by a couple of red-bereted soldiers. The MININT building is constantly photographed because of its signature Che Sculpture, but you don't want to go inside. I ignored the guards and strolled out onto the vast broken asphalt of the Plaza de la Revolución. On the far side, walking carefully, I cut past the entrance of a low but massive building sitting at the top of a sweeping driveway. This was the Council of State, the nucleus of the revolutionary system, where Raúl Castro oversaw his top functionaries. Special-forces troops with pistols and batons guarded the entrance ramp; the government feels secure enough that only a couple of pistols stood between me and Raúl.

Wandering, sometimes in circles, I passed out through Cerro and other neighborhoods until I found the house of Oswaldo Payá, one of Cuba's most important dissidents. We talked about politics, culture, neoliberalism, and human rights, but what caught my attention was his own personal economy. "My salary is 495 pesos a month," he said. "That's about ten meals for four or five people. Wages don't cover a fifth of our food needs. A 10-peso sandwich, with a 1-peso drink, is half my daily salary. With me going to my job and coming home, my three kids going to school, we spend about 12 pesos a day on transport—that's 50 to 60 percent of our total income." He himself survived thanks to a brother in Spain who sent money. "The paradox is that the workers are the poorest people in Cuba. We're all worse off than the guy who sells hot dogs in the gas station on the corner" (a hard currency enterprise). Most people had no CUC and went home hungry every night. "I don't say everything in Cuba is bad, or terrible. That's because we have distribution schemes to feed the poor, to give benefits. But that's another way of domination, keeping people eternally poor. Free my hands, I'll start a business and feed myself."

I asked him where someone would get the money for an iPod Touch, or any of the other gizmos, luxury goods, modern cars, sound systems, and sleek clothes that were increasingly common in Cuba. "A salary . . . is equal to poverty," he said. "They all have to rob the system to survive. That's the tolerated corruption of survival." A tiny middle class had emerged: "Businessmen, mostly ex-officials, people who run restaurants. All of them are regime people. Most are ex-military, or from the Ministry of the Exterior, and so on. They have connections. They are inside the system. They are untouchable." And there was a third, incredibly small but "indescribably" well-off group within the leadership, "with big houses, foreign travel, everything. The Cuban people know this group exists, but you will never see them, there is no way."

During an hour of talk, his wife, Ofelia, another human-rights activist and domestic servant, brought me a glass of pineapple juice. Oswaldo began to wrap up and urged me to come back for a meal and a mojito "anytime."

I stayed in my chair. All this talk of future meals had my mouth coursing with saliva. Ofelia saw this, and soon I heard frying in the kitchen.

We ate tomato soup, tomatoes, rice, and yellow lentils. She served some protein, a gray mash that I took for government picadillo because it tasted like soybeans and scraps of something that had once been an animal. But Ofelia dug the wrapper out of the garbage can. It was "mechanically separated" turkey meat from Cargill in the United States, part of the hundreds of millions of dollars' worth of agricultural products sold to Cuba every year under an exemption to the embargo. It was almost inedible, even in my hungry state, but Ofelia was beaming. "It's much better than the turkey we used to get," she said.

On the way out, Oswaldo tried to hand me 10 pesos. "Every Cuban would do this for you," he said. He told me to spend it on food, but I declined, pushing the bills away. I couldn't take cash from a source, though I didn't scruple at the meal. He insisted. In the end, to avoid walking home, I accepted a 1-peso coin for the bus.

Oswaldo walked me out through his gritty neighborhood, full of staring adolescent boys, to a bus stop. "Wear long pants" was his final advice. Only tourists went around in shorts.

I'd long ago finished my whiskey, and I was hard-pressed to enjoy Cuba without a drink. Oswaldo Payá had put the bug in my ear, declaring, "Having a drink is one of the rights we all have." It was time to make some liquor.

The only food I possessed in superabundance was sugar—I hadn't even bothered to pick up my allotment of "crude" sugar, because in three weeks I'd gone less than halfway through my four and a half pounds of refined white sugar. The process of making rum is simple, at least in theory. Sugar plus yeast equals alcohol. Distillation equals stronger alcohol. I had never distilled before, but I'd recently toured the Bushmills distillery in Northern Ireland and, fortified by notes from *Chasing the White Dog*, by Max Watman, I blundered my way toward bliss.

The first step was making a wash, or low-alcohol solution. I already had the sugar. I walked to the free bakery, where a disappointed crowd was waiting for the machines to turn out a new batch of bread. At the back door I flagged down a baker and asked if I could buy some yeast. "No," she said. "We don't have enough ourselves." In the now-familiar ritual, I hung out for a while, chatted her up, and soon she was shoving half a bag of yeast—made in England—through the fence. I tried to pay her, but she refused.

After reverse-engineering Watman's prose with a calculator, and converting to metric, I could only hope I was in the ballpark. A kilo of sugar would require slightly more than a gallon of water. In true Havana style, the water proved the biggest obstacle: tap water in the city is thick with magnesium. My landlord had a Korean water purifier, but it was broken. It took thirty-six hours to scrounge a single gallon of purified water. Then I scrubbed out my pressure cooker, tested and repaired its rubber seals, sterilized it, and dumped the water and sugar in. Watman didn't mention how much yeast to use; I went with "half," on the theory that a screw up would still leave me enough for a second shot.

Mix, close, wait. In four hours the pressure cooker—The-One-Fidel-Gave-Us—was almost bubbling over with scummy brown foam that smelled deadly. Distilling requires a hose. I tried a large hardware store in a hard currency shopping mall on the Malecón, then a hardware *shopping*, and finally asked a gas-station attendant. He told me to look for a man standing by a small card table on 3rd Avenue. After much discussion of alcohol, this grease-covered man, a black-market plumber straight out of *Brazil*, gave me a yard of filthy plastic tubing. I spent two hours trying to clean hardened grease out of this tube. Heat, soap, a rag, and a disarranged coat hanger made no dent. I couldn't have my booze tasting like an old Chevy.

Finally I asked a gardener working on a neighbor's yard if he could *conseguir* me a bit of tubing appropriate for distilling firewater. He thought this request the most natural thing in the world and returned in half an hour, having lopped off a yard of somebody's garden hose.

For the next two days I checked the pond scum in the cooker. It attracted fruit flies and gave off a gentle hiss.

The gods were smiling, and so were the prostitutes. For more than a week I had been fending off the attentions of a young lady who walked past my apartment. She was a classic example of the Cuban economy in action: hot pants, gold chains, blue eye shadow, platform sandals, and inch-long acrylic fingernails painted the colors of the Cuban flag.

"*Psst,*" she would say, calling my attention to these attributes. I often sat outside my small apartment to relieve the feeling of being trapped indoors. She would look through the iron gate along the road and summon me. *Psst.*

I resisted. But she was, like the many Cuban prostitutes I have talked with, a charming and intelligent survivor beneath the blunt *jewwannafuckeefuckee* propositions. We spoke once, then again a few days later, and then our third conversation lasted a long time. She kept trying to get into my apartment—did I have a light for her cigarette? Some coffee? a beer or soft drink?—and I kept stringing her along, enjoying her tales.

Her cleavage started ringing once, and she pulled out a cell phone. A tendentious conversation followed, in English. When she hung up she said, "He wants to fuck me in the ass." *Cogerme en el culo.* Cubans, especially prostitutes, are direct about sex. Also race. "Black guys always want to do it in the ass," she continued. "I don't like black guys, even though I consider myself black. I'm the lightest in my family, my mother is black, my sister is black, but I think black people smell bad. That guy has a lot of money. He's some kind of big man in the Cayman Islands, he's really rich. He offered me $150, but I told him no. Now he says he's going to pay me $300 just to have dinner."

"I don't think so," I observed.

"I know. I keep telling him to call my cousin. She loves black guys."

All our conversations began and ended with a proposition. Because, over a week, I had repeatedly turned her down, she now said, "I thought you were a duck." A what? "You know, *maricón. Un gay. Homosexual.*"

She was a nurse, twenty-four, from Holguín. She worked twelve hour shifts to earn vacation time, then every four or six months came to Havana for a long break to "dedicate myself to this," she said. In a rare euphemism, she said she was a *dama de acompañamiento.*

"Most of the girls have pimps, you know, but not me, so I have to look after myself." In addition to a phone, her cleavage concealed a small serrated knife, which she snapped open and waved around.

"You know why we do this," she said, "right? It's the only way to survive. I have a daughter, I love her so much, she's precious. I miss her. So I do this for her. Why don't you give me a hundred and I'll come upstairs right now?" (Eventually she offered me the "Cuban price" of $50.)

I told her I didn't have any money. I explained what I was doing. The ration. The salary. That I had already lost ten pounds. "I don't have a peso," I told her. She asked for a pen, wrote down her phone number, and handed it to me. Then she pulled, from one of the minuscule pockets of her hot pants, a single peso coin, which she handed to me.

"That's so you can call me," she said.

That was another terrible day for food, the worst yet. Between dawn and midnight I ate rice, beans, and sugar that totaled just over a thousand calories. I got up at three the next morning and finished the rice. Nothing left but a fistful of beans, two sweet potatoes, a few tiny plantains, three eggs, and a quarter of a cabbage.

Nine days to go.

I went to the ration shop, found Jesús, and bought coffee, a pound of rice, and some bread, all at Cuban prices—14 pesos total, or about 60 cents. That was the end of the money. But with the scraps of food, and the generosity of various Cubans, and a stomach shrunk to the size of a walnut, it would be enough. I knew I was going to make it.

I walked the next day to the house of Elizardo Sánchez, the human rights activist. An hour and ten minutes each way. "Everything is fine now," I told him, delirious with low blood sugar. "Even the prostitutes are giving me money."

I was in his house for an hour. He offered me a glass of water.

At last the great day of escape was here. Not my departure, which was still eight days away, but the alcohol. The brown wash had stopped bubbling after four days—when the alcohol content reaches about 13 percent it kills off the remaining yeast. I sterilized the garden hose and, using a bent hanger, fixed it to the vent on top of the pressure cooker. I struck a match, and in ten minutes I had alcohol vapor, and then a steady drip of condensation into the empty whiskey bottle sitting in a bowl of ice.

Ignorant, and a disgrace to my Virginia roots, I cooked the wash too hot and failed to throw away the initial stripping run of low wine—a harsh and even toxic alcohol. But after four hours the heart run had produced a liter of milky booze, and I had the naive sense to quit before the dregs could poison it. I should have made a second distillation, a spirit run, but couldn't be bothered. At four in the afternoon I finally sat down with a glass of warm white dog.

Thirty seconds after I started drinking I had a stomachache. The alcohol content was low, but so was my tolerance, and I was quickly giggling. The gardener came by and tasted some, with a sad face. I woke up at midnight with a headache, and this pattern continued for the last week of my residence. Instant stomachache; mild drunk; headache. The two or three hours in the middle were well worth it. When I left Havana there wasn't a drop of lightning left.

There wasn't much of me left either. In mid-February I walked one last time to the Riviera, weighing myself in the gym. I was down eleven and a half pounds since my arrival. More than eleven pounds gone in thirty days. I'd missed about 40,000 calories. At this rate I would be as lean as a Cuban by spring. And dead by autumn.

I finished out with a few tiny meals—the last of the ugly rice, a last sweet potato, and the quarter of a cabbage. On the day before my departure I broke into my emergency stash, eating the sesame sticks from the airplane (60 calories), and opening the can of fruit punch I'd smuggled in from the Bahamas (180). The taste of this red liquid was a shock: bitter with ascorbic acid, and flooded with sugar, to imitate the flavors of real juice. It was like drinking plastic.

My total expenditures on food were $15.08 for the month. By the end I'd read nine books, two of them about a thousand pages long, and written much of this article. I'd been living on the wages of a Cuban intellectual, and, indeed, I always write better, or at least faster, when I'm broke. My final morning: no breakfast, on top of no dinner. I used the prostitute's coin to catch a bus out toward the airport. I had to walk the last 45 minutes to my terminal, almost fainting on the way. There was a tragicomic moment when I was pulled out of line at the metal detectors by men in uniform because an immigration officer thought

I had overstayed my thirty-day visa. It took three people, repeatedly counting it out on their fingers, to prove that I was still on day thirty.

I ate a dinner and a breakfast in the Bahamas and gained four pounds. Back in the States, I put on another seven before the month was out. Put on nationality, change weight.

End Notes

1   For their protection from the Cuban state, certain persons in this article will go unnamed.

2   Cuba has two currencies, the valuable peso, officially called the CUC, and known as the kook, fula, chavita, and convertible; it was introduced to eliminate the presence of foreign currency and to be valued roughly equivalent to the U.S. dollar, at least before the 20 percent exchange fee. Then there is the lowly peso (known as the peso). Cubans are paid in the regular peso, and to get anything important they must trade twenty-four of these for one CUC. A tiny box of stir-fried noodles in Havana's Chinatown was priced at "75/2.5," in regular pesos and CUC, in either case representing about 15 percent of the average monthly income.

3   Those Cubans who ignore the summons to official labor can be charged with "dangerousness," a vague offense punishable by up to four years in jail. Dangerousness is "pre-crime," Elizardo Sánchez said—the police nipping your bad attitude in the bud before you have a chance to commit an actual crime. There are regular campaigns to arrest young people who try to avoid work or the draft, and this year it was particularly relentless, a sign of nervousness. "It's not easy to hide from the government," Sánchez told me. "Boys are required to register themselves for military service at fifteen. They change their address sometimes, but it doesn't work. It's very hard for a young person to hide. Cuba is a dossier society. From first grade onward, the police stop children and ask for I.D. They can radio in and get everything."

1. In what ways are Cuba's rations comparable to the U.S.'s government food programs? How are they different?

2. Is it better to have rations that must be supplemented through criminal income or to have a portion of the population that receives less than the equivalent of Cuba's rations?

3. What has influenced Cuba to keep its rationing program intact longer than other countries around the world?

Yasmin Alibhai-Brown is a British journalist and author and a regular columnist for the British newspapers The Independent *and* The Evening Standard. *Born in Uganda to an East African mother and an Indian father, she chose to immigrate to Britain before Idi Amin began his campaign against Ugandan Asians. Alibhai-Brown studied philosophy at Oxford University and is now known for her writing related to issues of race, ethnicity, multiculturalism, diversity, and immigration.*

HOORAY FOR BOLLYWOOD: 100 YEARS OF INDIAN CINEMA

By Yasmin Alibhai-Brown

The Indian film industry is the biggest and loudest on the planet. Eight hundred films are produced every year for domestic audiences of a billion-plus and a burgeoning overseas market. Although regional and independent films have always done their own thing, and brilliantly, the most prodigious sector is Bollywood, the ultimate dream factory in Mumbai.

Burhan Wazir, director of the Doha Film Institute, finds the films formulaic, featuring "gym-fit actors, exotic locations and rampantly consumerist lifestyles." Which is true, but it is such a winning formula that glitzy Bollywood is now outshining Hollywood—no mean feat, when one considers how American cultural hegemony has dominated and disabled the European film industries.

Beautiful megastars Shah Rukh Khan and Aishwarya Rai appear on the covers of *Forbes* and *Time* magazine and are considered more famous globally than Tom Cruise or Julia Roberts. Michael Ellis of the Motion Picture Association admits that U.S. studios have not penetrated the Indian market. Until 2008, American cinemas did not screen Hindi movies. Now they do, big time.

In Los Angeles, dance studios teach Bollywood dancing to wannabe starlets while Columbia, Disney, Fox et al. seek out co-production deals with Bollywood. Hitherto narcissistic Hollywood was oblivious to its eastern counterpart. Now it is sprinting to catch up with the rest of the world. Bollywood patriarch and superstar Amitabh Bachchan is jubilant that they who ignored or ridiculed his industry are eating humble (American) pie: "We always knew and believed in our films. The uniqueness of Hindi cinema has been its content... It has survived almost 100 years and is still growing [so] it must be doing something right."

So what is the secret of this success? According to the buoyant director Karan Johar, it is, "A mixture of music, love, family values, comedy, fantasy... [and an] adventurous choice of film location." Discerning audiences know that films are not real life but allegories which give hope because good triumphs over evil, poetic justice prevails.

Nasreen Munni Kabir, curator of Channel 4's annual season of Hindi movies, writes: "They are unquestionably the most-seen movies in the world... [watched] well beyond the Indian continent and the diaspora, in such unlikely places as Russia, China, the Middle East, the Far East, Turkey and Africa. People from very different cultural and social worlds have a great love for Indian popular cinema, and many have been Hindi film fans for over 50 years." Mao Tse-tung was a fan, as were millions of others in communist countries. Bollywood was a globalised phenomenon long before our age of globalisation.

It all started exactly 100 years ago when DJ Phalke, a nerdy-looking, bespectacled Indian Brahmin made the first ever Indian feature film, *Raja Harishchandra*, about a noble king guided by Hindu gods, some frolicsome, some deadly and full of wrath.

In 1895, the French Lumière brothers had created the first motion pictures, and by 1911, moving images had been shown in Mumbai venues, creating a buzz and palpable anticipation. A vast audience was prepped for this new medium, its possibilities and magic, and Phalke's first big filmic adventure. He became king of the silent era, producing dozens of mythological films with actors gesticulating wildly, backed by some live music and crude sound effects. The film-maker was populist and subversive, a storyteller with messianic resolve.

Let us go back to India in 1912. The British Raj was full of pomp and hubris, and natives were getting restive. Two years later, Gandhi would launch his liberation movement. Phalke had studied art and architecture, tried printing, photography, archaeology and various other ventures. And then, in Mumbai, he watched a French film, *The Life of Christ*, and was gripped "by a strange spell. I bought another ticket and saw the film again. Could we, the sons of India, ever be able to see Indian images on the screen?" He had found his calling. He would put those images on screen to awaken Indian nationalism.

Ironically, however, Phalke knew he couldn't fulfil his mission without western technology and British expertise. He travelled to Europe, met directors, bought a Williamson camera and, in London, was trained by the English director Cecil Hepworth in his Walton-on-Thames studios. Creative Indian and European film-makers then were mutually respectful collaborators who circumvented political partition, defied colonial and societal strictures.

Phalke thrilled audiences and subliminally aroused his compatriots to resist unjust power and inequality. Other silent films chose their own targets. As early as 1921, *England Returned* mocked pretentious, Anglicised Indians. (*Goodness Gracious Me* picked on similar characters in their hit BBC TV series in the 1990s.) Risqué and sexually daring films seemed to herald new personal freedoms. One of the boldest was *Shiraz* (1928), about ill-fated, royal lovers, directed by Franz Osten, a German. The producer and leading actor was the Indian trailblazer, Himansu Rai. It was shown in Germany and England to great acclaim.

Fearing films could incite dissidence and high emotion, colonial administrators imposed strict censorship. Any character wearing a loin cloth was deemed dangerous because it was Gandhi's chosen attire; so, too, any expression of patriotism. To beat the bans, anti-British messages were embedded in song lyrics. Post-imperial India kept the scissors and state censorship. The Brits cut seditious messages; Indian controllers expurgated "licentiousness"—kisses and bedroom antics. So smart directors used dance and suggestive dialogue to make highly charged, erotic films. Just don't tell the censors.

Gorgeous Devika Rani, an Indian actress trained at Rada, met Rai in London in 1928, married him and starred in his films. One of these, *Karma* (1933), was in English, shot in a London studio and premiered in Leicester Square. Rani received rave reviews, but the film bombed, and the couple moved back home. Two years earlier, the sound era had arrived with Alam Ara, a historical musical made by Ardeshir Irani, and Rai and Rani, the hot and ambitious couple, set up the Bombay Talkies studio. One of its early hits was *Achhut Kanya*, about untouchables, starring Rani and directed by Osten, who made 18 films in India—yet joined the Nazi Party while doing so. Inexplicable.

Lalit Mohan Joshi, founder of the South Asian Cinema Foundation in London, was born in India, and used to bunk off school to sneak into cinemas, like the boy in *Cinema Paradiso*. He tells me that in the 1930s and 1940s, common themes were female rights, hypocritical social mores and caste prejudice, always done beautifully through compelling stories and acting.

Idealistic and artistic directors won prizes at Cannes and Venice. They used the popular art form to create unity in a multilingual, disparate, often conflicted nation. Muslims were key players, and astonishingly, Jewish and Christian actresses—some European—were employed by the studios, usually to play red-lipped vamps. The influence of cinema in India, says Joshi, is immeasurable: "It has more of an impact than books, art and even religion."

Adulated stars join the limitless pantheon of Hindu deities. When Bachchan was seriously injured while filming in 1982, millions stopped work, fasted and prayed. PM Indira Gandhi cancelled a foreign trip to go to his bedside. Shah Rukh, Aamir and Salman Khan (unrelated) are today's top male idols. All three are of Muslim heritage and immensely powerful. Aamir created and hosts a TV programme which confronts unjust and corrupt practices in public and domestic life. Six hundred million people watch the show, which terrifies and chastens the powerful and rich. Several Bollywood luminaries have gone into politics.

The golden age of Hindi cinema was, arguably, from the 1950s to the mid-1960s. And again, British technical expertise was enlisted by some celebrated Indian producers. Among the actors who emerged then were Prithviraj Kapoor and his sons Raj, Shammi and Shashi; also, Dev Anand, Dilip Kumar and, among others, Raj Kapoor, also a director, replicated Chaplin's hapless characters in memorable films. The Kapoor acting dynasty is still going strong in Bollywood.

Wonderful actresses such as Nargis and Waheeda Rehman (both Muslims), Meena Kumari and Geeta Bali, meanwhile, were not always good, obedient Asian women. They were rule-breakers, some mistresses and hard drinkers in real life, all defiant and free on screen. Nargis wore revealing ballgowns and short tennis skirts and played feisty characters.

In the remarkable film *Guide* (1965), Rehman, a dancer, was stuck with an archaeologist husband much like Casaubon in *Middlemarch*. A sexy tourist guide came along and the heroine went off with him. That, though, didn't end her deep unhappiness. In her most famous film *Pakeezah* (1972), Meena Kumari played a dignified courtesan exposing society's duplicities.

Moral concerns were depicted with such feeling that they stayed with you, within you. The Oscar-shortlisted *Mother India* (1957) was about tough, maternal love and the unwinnable fight for peasant land rights. The usually glam Nargis played the heroine. That powerful drama seeded my socialist principles. In 1960, another immortal masterpiece was released—*Mughal-e-Azam*, about a Mughal prince and a dancing girl, an epic tussle between love and duty. My English husband has watched it five times.

From the late 1960s, Bollywood changed, perhaps forever. Flamboyant films arrived, with ridiculous story-lines, foreign locations, lovers running around trees and gyrating women breaking into song and dance for no good reason. And bad jokes. Movies such as *An Evening in Paris* and *Love in Tokyo* were cringe-making but box-office hits. Then in the 1970s, came the Indian Rambo, ballsy Bachchan, playing volcanic young men and breaking all box-office records. The actor seemed to channel the people's anger under the authoritarian PM Indira Gandhi.

Through the good and bad times, India's independent sector has produced internationally lauded films with low budgets. Satyajit Ray, of course, and Shyam Benegal, Aparna Sen (an actress too, who starred in Ray's films), Mrinal Sen and others have made classics without Bollywood's razzmatazz. Benegal's *Ankur* starred the subtle and versatile actress, Shabana Azmi, who played an adulterous wife. It is among my 10 favourite films.

Modern director Onir, famous for his touching films on homosexuality and other taboo subjects, has compared Bollywood to a shopping mall, calling it mindless and regressive, and is part of a confident new wave which is making its mark at home and internationally. As are diasporic Indian film-makers such as Mira Nair (*Salaam Bombay!*, *Monsoon Wedding*, *The Reluctant Fundamentalist*) and Deepa Mehta, director of Rushdie's *Midnight's Children*.

For post-war Asian migrants to the UK, Hindi movies were cheap entertainment and gave them solace, an identity as they coped with racism and dreadful weather. The multi-talented Meera Syal remembers going to Hindi films at Wolverhampton picturehouses with her family: "This was the only time and place we saw an art form that was ours. People dressed up and it was as exciting as it must have been for Elizabethan audiences going to the theatre. It was a window into a country I didn't really know, a living link. And I felt proud. To see people who looked like us acting and dancing was amazing. Remember, TV here then had no place for us. The films also had good messages—about families being sacred."

Gurinder Chadha, renowned director of *Bend it Like Beckham* and *Bride & Prejudice*, was brought up in Southall and went on Sundays with her family to the temple, then a Bollywood film—"The singing and dancing, big musical numbers, bright colours, big emotions!"—followed by samosas and sweets at a local café. She too admires early Hindi films because they had social commentary and defiant messages, all dressed up with songs and music: "A lot of it was about installing pride and unity in this new, freshly independent nation. They were trying to define who they were."

The kitsch came later and carries on, but every decade, she believes, has produced remarkable films reflecting political, economic and social shifts and moods. Interestingly, Chadha's best work is influencing some Indians in the business.

So where are we now? In the words of the novelist Hari Kunzru, "Bollywood has taken a contemporary turn and production values often overshadow narrative. Social-conscience movies dissolved during the 1980s into a torrid orgy of wet-sari clad violence and were overtaken by a new generation of super-glossy love stories with big budgets and international locations."

I tire of the bling and Lamborghinis, the vast mansions, super-lavish weddings and in-house gods covered in real gold leaf. Joshi, too, finds these developments disheartening: "Most of today's films are not deep. They are pseudo, plastic, have no originality or integrity. Whereas before, directors were progressive, today they are regressive." He is right: previously movie-makers were unabashedly Indian, used their own idiom, with integrity and without trying too hard to impress or emulate America or Europe.

Modern global capitalism has changed all that. Indians in the US and UK are upwardly mobile, über-aspirational and getting wealthy. They disdain moralising stories about dirt-poor rural Indian villagers or oppressed women. In India itself, too, the rapidly growing urban middle- and upper-classes want movies which cast them as heroes of a brave new world, not tearful folk tales.

In India this January, the shrill daughter of a wealthy financier gave me an earful: "I mean, you arty types like all those sad films with the poor and weeping women and all that. Why? Is it that you can't accept that India is now a superpower? That you want us to stay backward for your entertainment? Why do you hate and mock Indians who walk tall in Jimmy Choos?" Maybe she has a point. Are those who fetishise old, socially concerned movies refusing to acknowledge, new, shining India? Perhaps, but only because those old divides and injustices have become worse.

And anyway, there is no turning back: Bollywood in the 21st century is a rising brand. Of 12 white students interviewed at Middlesex University for this article, most recognised the "product" and big names and some had watched the movies. That never happened before. Of the Asian students also interviewed, trendy and irreversibly British, almost all watched the films and felt affirmed by them, just as Syal did way, way back.

Though there is too much dross, Bollywood has, in this decade, been making movies of real substance, displaying innovation, high production values, courage and artistry. Examples include *Omkara*, based on *Othello*, a multi-layered film of the destructive love between a gullible outlaw and his lover from a respectable family; and *Barfi!*, a story of a dumb-and-deaf charmer, the highest-grossing movie in India in 2012. The most highly paid stars are now choosing to act in non-glam films with meaning.

So the future looks bright. My American friend, married to an Indian, is unsettled by that: "These movies are great, but they tell me power is moving away from the U.S., going east. And you know that's hard for us Americans." Her husband cut in, "It's time things were hard for you all. Hollywood will be humbled by Bollywood. Watch this space." Someone should make a movie about the clash of these two titans.

1. In the article, Alibhai-Brown discusses some Indian filmmakers' perceptions that Bollywood has become "mindless" and "regressive," and that the influence of globalization and commercialism has degraded the film industry. In 2013, American director Stephen Soderbergh gave a keynote address to the San Francisco Film Festival, in which he decried similar problems in American, Hollywood cinema. After listening to Soderbergh's speech, do you see explicit connections between the two industries? Do the problems share a common source, or do these problems and complaints spring from different sources and bear differing results?

   http://www.indiewire.com/article/watch-full-video-recording-of-steven-soderberghs-impassioned-state-of-cinema-address-from-the-san-francisco-film-festival

2. Alibhai-Brown quotes many in the Indian Film Industry who fear that materialistic, spectacular depictions of Indian culture and life in Bollywood films are degrading and should give way to films that tackle social realism. However, others argue that the spectacle in these films is part of what has made them popular with global audiences and helped the industry to grow. Would abandoning this spectacle help or harm the industry? Do these considerations play out differently for an emerging industry than they would for Hollywood?

Jon Kelly is the feature writer for the BBC News. He has previously reported for Guardian, Observer, Daily Record, The Scotsman, The Tablet, *and* The List. *He was educated at City University and the University of Edinburgh in Britain. He has an honors Masters in Politics and was awarded Critic of the Year from* Guardian Student Media Awards *in 2000.*

WHY BRITISH POLICE DON'T HAVE GUNS

By Jon Kelly

The deaths of two female police constables have brought into focus the unarmed status of most British police. Why does Britain hold firm against issuing guns to officers on the beat?

It's the single most obvious feature that sets the British bobby apart from their counterparts overseas.

Tourists and visitors regularly express surprise at the absence of firearms from the waists of officers patrolling the streets.

But to most inhabitants of the UK—with the notable exception of Northern Ireland—it is a normal, unremarkable state of affairs that most front-line officers do not carry guns.

Unremarkable, that is, until unarmed officers like Nicola Hughes and Fiona Bone are killed in the line of duty. There are always those who question why Britain is out of step with most of the rest of the world, with the exceptions of the Republic of Ireland, New Zealand, Norway and a handful of other nations.

VIEW FROM A BOBBY

A police constable serving in a city in southern England gives his view:

"I have been in the police for 12 years, before that I was in the Army. I would happily carry a gun if the decision was made but it won't ever happen.

"I don't think practically it could work because of the training. Officers in this country are highly trained and this would extend to firearms training, too. But, at the moment, with all the cuts, we can't put enough officers in the cars, let alone give them firearms training.

"Also, the police in this country are always under so much scrutiny. Look at the issue of Tasers, the civil liberty groups think they are one of the most inhumane things going.

"I was previously injured badly in an assault. My colleague and I feared for our lives—thankfully other officers came to our aid. I don't think a gun—or a Taser for that matter—would have helped us in that situation. Communication is one of the best tools, and to be honest, having a gun could make an officer feel over-confident."

For a heavily urbanised country of its population size, the situation in Great Britain is arguably unique.

Film director Michael Winner, founder of the Police Memorial Trust, and Tony Rayner, the former chairman of Essex Police Federation, have both called for officers to be routinely armed.

But despite the loss of two of his officers, Greater Manchester Chief Constable Sir Peter Fahy was quick to speak in support of the status quo.

"We are passionate that the British style of policing is routinely unarmed policing. Sadly we know from the experience in America and other countries that having armed officers certainly does not mean, sadly, that police officers do not end up getting shot."

But one thing is clear. When asked, police officers say overwhelmingly that they wish to remain unarmed.

A 2006 survey of 47,328 Police Federation members found 82% did not want officers to be routinely armed on duty, despite almost half saying their lives had been "in serious jeopardy" during the previous three years.

It is a position shared by the Police Superintendents' Association and the Association of Chief Police Officers.

The British public are not nearly so unanimous.

An ICM poll in April 2004 found 47% supported arming all police, compared with 48% against.

In 2007, the centre-right think-tank Policy Exchange found 72% of 2,156 adults wanted to see more armed police patrols.

INTERNATIONAL MODELS

All major police forces in Europe, as well as the U.S., Canada and Australia routinely carry firearms, says Prof. Peter Waddington. The exceptions are Britain, the Irish Republic, and New Zealand. In Norway, officers carry arms in their cars but not on their person, he says.

New Zealand has adopted an armed response model similar to Britain, says the International Law Enforcement Forum. There was considerable debate there in 2010 when two officers were shot, and commissioner Peter Marshall wrote: "International experience shows that making firearms more accessible raises certain risks that are very difficult to control."

These considerations included:

- risk of police having weapons taken from them
- risk of greater use of weapons against the public and/or offenders
- and ambush can never be controlled, whether or not officers are armed

For decades there have been incidents that have led to calls for issuing all officers with firearms. Cases like those of Sharon Beshenivsky, shot dead during a robbery in 2005, or of the three plain-clothes officers murdered by Harry Roberts in west London in 1966, or the killing of PC Sidney Miles in the Derek Bentley case of 1952.

Few expect the system to change even after widespread public horror at the deaths of PCs Bone and Hughes.

For one thing, incidents such as that in Greater Manchester are extremely rare. Overall gun crime, too, remains low.

In 2010-11, England and Wales witnessed 388 firearm offences in which there was a fatal or serious injury, 13% lower than the previous 12 months. In Scotland during the same period, there were two fatal and 109 non-fatal injuries during the same period, a decade-long low.

Additionally, officers, chief constables and politicians alike are wary of upsetting an equilibrium that has been maintained throughout Britain's 183-year policing history.

"There's a general recognition that if the police are walking around with guns it changes things," says Richard Garside, director of the Centre for Crime and Justice Studies.

Firearms offences in England and Wales 1969-2011

Total (thousands)

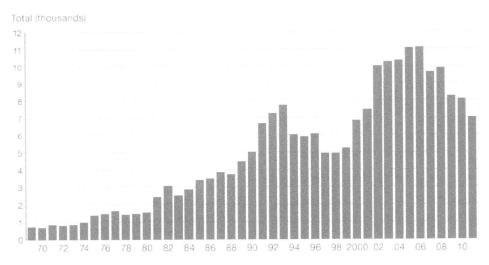

Source: Home Office

Arming the force would, say opponents, undermine the principle of policing by consent—the notion that the force owes its primary duty to the public, rather than to the state, as in other countries.

This owes much to the historical foundations of British criminal justice, says Peter Waddington, professor of social policy at the University of Wolverhampton.

"A great deal of what we take as normal about policing was set out in the early 19th century," he says.

POLICE USE OF FIREARMS 2010-11

- Authorized in 17,209 operations, says Home Office figures for England and Wales—a decrease of 1,347 (7%) on previous year

- 6,653 authorized firearms officers—(5% decrease)

- 13,346 operations involving armed response vehicles (6% decrease)

- Three incidents in which police discharged a conventional firearm (down from six incidents)

"When Robert Peel formed the Metropolitan Police there was a very strong fear of the military—the masses feared the new force would be oppressive."

A force that did not routinely carry firearms—and wore blue rather than red, which was associated with the infantry—was part of this effort to distinguish the early "Peelers" from the Army, Waddington says.

Over time, this notion of guns being inimical to community policing—and, indeed, to the popular conception of the Dixon of Dock Green-style bobby—was reinforced.

While some in London were issued with revolvers prior to 1936, from that date only trained officers at the rank of sergeant or above were issued with guns, and even then only if they could demonstrate a good reason for requiring one.

Today only a small proportion of officers are authorized to use firearms. Latest Home Office figures show there were just 6,653 officers authorized to use firearms in England and Wales—about 5% of the total number.

None of which implies, of course, that the British police are somehow gun-free. Each police force has its own firearms unit. Police armed response vehicles have been deployed since 1991.

VIEW FROM LOUISIANA

Colonel Richie Johnson West Baton Rouge Sheriff's Office

"What does a British police officer do if someone comes out with a knife? Is he supposed to get out his knife and fight him?

"Our citizens are armed—even the bad ones. The criminal element here is better armed than the police departments most of the times, due to budget constraints.

"It would be impossible for us to do our job if we weren't armed. I'd have to quit. I worked narcotics for 20 years and definitely in that field, how would you do that job without being armed? Even as a patrolman, you're reactive. The other guy knows what he's going to do. It definitely has to be armed when you have to be reactive.

"The public expects us to be armed—when they call in the cavalry that's exactly what they want. The general public, because of television, they believe that we're a lot better armed than we really are. You respond to a call and they say 'Where's your machine gun?'"

In addition, trained officers have had access to Tasers since 2004 despite controversy about their use. Met Commissioner Bernard Hogan-Howe called for police response officers to be routinely armed with the weapons in November 2011.

Particularly in London, the sight of armed officers at airports, embassies and other security-sensitive locations has become a familiar one, especially since the 11 September attacks.

However much firearms become an accepted part of British life, former Met deputy assistant commissioner Brian Paddick doubts police themselves will ever support a universal rollout.

For one thing, the sheer cost of equipping all personnel with weapons as well as providing regular training would be prohibitive at a time of public spending cuts, he says.

In addition, Paddick adds, front-line officers would not be keen to face the agonising, split-second decisions faced by their counterparts in specialist firearms units.

"In terms of the police being approachable, in terms of the public being the eyes and ears of the police, officers don't want to lose that," he says.

"Every case in which a police officer has shot someone brings it home to unarmed officers the sheer weight of responsibility that their colleagues face."

Cases like that of Jean Charles de Menezes, shot dead by a Met firearms officer after he was wrongly identified as a terrorist, illustrate Paddick's point.

For now, at least, that starkest of all distinctions between British officers and those abroad looks secure.

What are some of the recent societal attitudes that have contributed to the British population being in favor of armed police?

What is your reaction to the statement " . . . policing by consent— the notion that the [police] force owes its primary duty to the public, rather than to the state, as in other countries?"

Jamey Keaten currently writes for the Associated Press as their Paris correspondent. He specializes in politics, foreign affairs, defense, and security.

MUSLIMS WORRY ABOUT BROADER FRANCE HEADSCARF BAN

By Jamey Keaten

LE BOURGET, France—Because of her choice to wear a headscarf, Samia Kaddour, a Muslim, has all but abandoned trying to land a government job in France. Soon, some private sector jobs could be off limits, too.

French President Francois Hollande says he wants a new law that could extend restrictions on the wearing of prominent religious symbols in state jobs into the private sector. His new tack comes after a top French court ruled in March that a day care operator that gets some state funding unfairly fired a woman in a headscarf, sparking a political backlash.

As Christians celebrated Easter on Sunday, Kaddour attended the four-day Annual Meeting of Muslims of France in Le Bourget, north of Paris. The convention, which last year drew some 160,000 faithful and was expected to grow this year, is billed as the largest annual gathering of its kind in Europe. It is in its 30th year and ended Monday.

French law bars state employees from wearing prominent religious symbols such as Muslim headscarves, Jewish skullcaps or large Christian crosses in public schools, welfare offices or other government facilities. Two years ago, France banned Muslim veils that cover faces, such as the niqab, which has a slit for the eyes, or the mesh-screen burqa, from being worn anywhere in public.

Meeting leaders say France has made progress in accepting Muslims and noted that, unlike 30 years ago, women wearing headscarves today rarely draw suspicion, scowls or curiosity. Still, many Muslims—and even some Roman Catholics and Jews—fear France's insistence on secular values first enshrined in the French Revolution more than two centuries ago is unfairly crimping their ability to express their religious beliefs freely.

They also worry that Hollande's Socialist government, like a conservative one before it, wants to score political points.

"Islam has become a political instrument," said Kaddour, 26, who is a community activist from the English Channel port city of Le Havre and one of 10 children of Algerian-born parents who moved to France for plentiful jobs during its economic boom times decades ago. "Islam is always brandished whenever there is internal political discord."

Most mainstream politicians insist Islam is not being targeted. But a backlash erupted after the Court of Cassation ruled in March that Baby Loup, a private-sector day care operator that gets some state funding, unfairly fired a woman who wore a headscarf to work. The far-right railed at the decision, and even Interior Minister Manuel Valls expressed regret over it.

Wading into the debate in a prime-time TV interview on Thursday, Hollande suggested new limits are needed on Muslim headscarves, saying that "when there is contact with children, in what we call public service of early childhood ... there should be a certain similarity to what exists in (public) school.

"I think the law should get involved," he added.

Many Muslims fear an encroaching Islamophobia, while proponents of such measures insist they counter extremism and act as a rampart to protect France's identity against inequality. Polls show that most French people support at least some restrictions on religious symbols.

France, with an estimated 5 million-6 million Muslims whose families mostly have origins in former French colonies in north Africa, is at the forefront of addressing the challenges that many European countries are facing about how to integrate their sizeable ethnic and religious minorities on a continent where white Christians have dominated the political landscape for centuries.

Bristling against stereotypes in many corners of the West that Muslims are closet radicals or even terrorists, leaders of the convention in Le Bourget preached peace and justice. And after prayers and praise of Islam's Prophet Muhammad, convention leaders led a song in Arabic in a vast meeting hall with thousands in the audience — and some up on the dais waved French flags.

In another convention hall, vendors offered items such as headscarves, sweet pastries or T-shirts emblazoned with the saying 'Don't Panic, I'm Muslim,' while mothers pushing strollers and others wandered through the crowd. Several other stalls took up political issues such as support for Palestinians or war-weary Syrians. Nearby, men kneeled in rhythmic unison for afternoon prayers.

Kaddour said many Muslims regret that their faith is in the political crosscurrents again in France. But she said she's not discouraged enough yet to want to leave.

"Many others feel that way too: We are French and we have our place to claim and our future to establish in France," she said. "I'm not a foreigner. I'm French. I want to live in France; I love this country. Even if it has trouble liking us, we are going to do what's necessary to live serenely in France."

Kaddour says she plans to go back to school to get a higher degree but has all but given up hopes for a state job. And in France, that matters: the European Union says more than half of France's gross domestic product comes from government spending—potentially curbing the work options for headscarf-wearing Muslims such as Kaddour if the ban is broadened.

"A state job, unfortunately..." she said, her voice trailing off. "When I go into job interviews, I wear my headscarf. No results." She admits that she doesn't always know why—it could just be her skill set isn't sufficient—but suspects her religion plays a role, too.

Kaddour says her future career seems increasingly limited to independent, private practice work. She currently works for a small community group devoted to improving understanding of Islam, called Le Havre de Savoir, or The Haven of Knowledge.

At a time of double-digit unemployment rates in France, a nation of 65 million, such restrictions to job access hit headscarf-wearing women especially hard: Muslim men in France don't usually wear visible religious garb.

Ahmed Jaballah, the head of the Union of Islamic Organizations of France, a major Muslim group that helped organize the conference, said the "rather morose ambiance" over France's sluggish economic growth recently hasn't helped Muslims' aspirations, suggesting that a search for scapegoats is politically appealing. He said he's concerned about the government's plans.

"Unfortunately, Muslims have the impression today that secularism is being shaped based on Muslim practices, and that's worrisome," he said in an interview. "Everybody always talks about secularism, how it's not just about Muslims. But in fact, Muslims are targeted. Nobody is fooled.

"Muslims wonder: Can we trust secularism?" he said. "Remember the French slogan: 'Liberte, Egalite, Fraternite.' Today, we want this fraternity to be real."

1. Should headscarves be banned in all businesses, federal and private?

2. Using the "Cui Bono" handout, describe the gains and losses and the groups involved if France legally bans religious symbols from private businesses. Then do the same if these religious symbols are not banned.

Anu Partanen is a Finnish journalist, freelance writer, visiting reporter, and columnist based in New York City. She has written for the New York Times and The Atlantic and has been a visiting staff writer for Helsingin Sanomat, Scandinavia's largest daily subscription newspaper. Anu Partanen holds a master's degree in Social Science and has studied in France and Australia. She is married to the American writer and educator, Trevor Corson.

WHAT AMERICANS KEEP IGNORING ABOUT FINLAND'S SCHOOL SUCCESS

By Anu Partanen

The Scandinavian country is an education superpower because it values equality more than excellence.

Everyone agrees the United States needs to improve its education system dramatically, but how? One of the hottest trends in education reform lately is looking at the stunning success of the West's reigning education superpower, Finland. Trouble is, when it comes to the lessons that Finnish schools have to offer, most of the discussion seems to be missing the point.

The small Nordic country of Finland used to be known—if it was known for anything at all—as the home of Nokia, the mobile phone giant. But lately Finland has been attracting attention on global surveys of quality of life—*Newsweek* ranked it number one last year—and Finland's national education system has been receiving particular praise, because in recent years Finnish students have been turning in some of the highest test scores in the world.

Finland's schools owe their newfound fame primarily to one study: the PISA survey, conducted every three years by the Organization for Economic Co-operation and Development (OECD). The survey compares 15-year-olds in different countries in reading, math, and science. Finland has ranked at or near the top in all three competencies on every survey since 2000, neck and neck with superachievers such as South Korea and Singapore. In the most recent survey in 2009 Finland slipped slightly, with students in Shanghai, China, taking the best scores, but the Finns are still near the very top. Throughout the same period, the PISA performance of the United States has been middling, at best.

Compared with the stereotype of the East Asian model—long hours of exhaustive cramming and rote memorization—Finland's success is especially intriguing because Finnish schools assign less homework and engage children in more creative play. All this has led to a continuous stream of foreign delegations making the pilgrimage to Finland to visit schools and talk with the nation's education experts, and constant coverage in the worldwide media marveling at the Finnish miracle.

So there was considerable interest in a recent visit to the U.S. by one of the leading Finnish authorities on education reform, Pasi Sahlberg, director of the Finnish Ministry of Education's Center for International Mobility and author of the new book *Finnish Lessons: What Can the World Learn from Educational Change in Finland?* Earlier this month, Sahlberg stopped by the Dwight School in New York City to speak with educators and students, and his visit received national media attention and generated much discussion.

And yet it wasn't clear that Sahlberg's message was actually getting through. As Sahlberg put it to me later, there are certain things nobody in America really wants to talk about.

* * * * *

During the afternoon that Sahlberg spent at the Dwight School, a photographer from the *New York Times* jockeyed for position with Dan Rather's TV crew as Sahlberg participated in a roundtable chat with students. The subsequent article in the *Times* about the event would focus on Finland as an "intriguing school-reform model."

Yet one of the most significant things Sahlberg said passed practically unnoticed. "Oh," he mentioned at one point, "and there are no private schools in Finland."

This notion may seem difficult for an American to digest, but it's true. Only a small number of independent schools exist in Finland, and even they are all publicly financed. None is allowed to charge tuition fees. There are no private universities, either. This means that practically every person in Finland attends public school, whether for pre-K or a Ph.D.

The irony of Sahlberg's making this comment during a talk at the Dwight School seemed obvious. Like many of America's best schools, Dwight is a private institution that costs high-school students upward of $35,000 a year to attend—not to mention that Dwight, in particular, is run for profit, an increasing trend in the U.S. Yet no one in the room commented on Sahlberg's statement. I found this surprising. Sahlberg himself did not.

Sahlberg knows what Americans like to talk about when it comes to education, because he's become their go-to guy in Finland. The son of two teachers, he grew up in a Finnish school. He taught mathematics and physics in a junior high school in Helsinki, worked his way through a variety of positions in the Finnish Ministry of Education, and spent years as an education expert at the OECD, the World Bank and other international organizations.

Now, in addition to his other duties, Sahlberg hosts about a hundred visits a year by foreign educators, including many Americans, who want to know the secret of Finland's success. Sahlberg's new book is partly an attempt to help answer the questions he always gets asked.

From his point of view, Americans are consistently obsessed with certain questions: How can you keep track of students' performance if you don't test them constantly? How can you improve teaching if you have no accountability for bad teachers or merit pay for good teachers? How do you foster competition and engage the private sector? How do you provide school choice?

The answers Finland provides seem to run counter to just about everything America's school reformers are trying to do.

For starters, Finland has no standardized tests. The only exception is what's called the National Matriculation Exam, which everyone takes at the end of a voluntary upper-secondary school, roughly the equivalent of American high school.

Instead, the public school system's teachers are trained to assess children in classrooms using independent tests they create themselves. All children receive a report card at the end of each semester, but these reports are based on individualized grading by each teacher. Periodically, the Ministry of Education tracks national progress by testing a few sample groups across a range of different schools.

As for accountability of teachers and administrators, Sahlberg shrugs. "There's no word for accountability in Finnish," he later told an audience at the Teachers College of Columbia University. "Accountability is something that is left when responsibility has been subtracted."

For Sahlberg, what matters is that in Finland all teachers and administrators are given prestige, decent pay, and a lot of responsibility. A master's degree is required to enter the profession, and teacher training programs are among the most selective professional schools in the country. If a teacher is bad, it is the principal's responsibility to notice and deal with it.

And while Americans love to talk about competition, Sahlberg points out that nothing makes Finns more uncomfortable. In his book, Sahlberg quotes a line from Finnish writer named Samuli Paronen: "Real winners do not compete." It's hard to think of a more un-American idea, but when it comes to education, Finland's success shows that the Finnish attitude might have merits. There are no lists of best schools or teachers in Finland. The main driver of education policy is not competition between teachers and between schools, but cooperation.

Finally, in Finland, school choice is noticeably not a priority, nor is engaging the private sector at all. Which brings us back to the silence after Sahlberg's comment at the Dwight School that schools like Dwight don't exist in Finland.

"Here in America," Sahlberg said at the Teachers College, "parents can choose to take their kids to private schools. It's the same idea of a marketplace that applies to, say, shops. Schools are a shop and parents can buy what ever they want. In Finland parents can also choose. But the options are all the same."

Herein lay the real shocker. As Sahlberg continued, his core message emerged, whether or not anyone in his American audience heard it.

Decades ago, when the Finnish school system was badly in need of reform, the goal of the program that Finland instituted, resulting in so much success today, was never excellence. It was equity.

* * * * *

Since the 1980s, the main driver of Finnish education policy has been the idea that every child should have exactly the same opportunity to learn, regardless of family background, income, or geographic location. Education has been seen first and foremost not as a way to produce star performers but as an instrument to even out social inequality.

In the Finnish view, as Sahlberg describes it, this means that schools should be healthy, safe environments for children. This starts with the basics. Finland offers all pupils free school meals, easy access to health care, psychological counseling, and individualized student guidance.

In fact, since academic excellence wasn't a particular priority on the Finnish to-do list, when Finland's students scored so high on the first PISA survey in 2001, many Finns thought the results must be a mistake. But subsequent PISA tests confirmed that Finland—unlike, say, very similar countries such as Norway—was producing academic excellence through its particular policy focus on equity.

That this point is almost always ignored or brushed aside in the U.S. seems especially poignant at the moment, after the financial crisis and Occupy Wall Street movement have brought the problems of inequality in America into such sharp focus. The chasm between those who can afford $35,000 in tuition per child per year—or even just the price of a house in a good public school district—and the other "99 percent" is painfully plain to see.

* * * * *

Pasi Sahlberg goes out of his way to emphasize that his book *Finnish Lessons* is not meant as a how-to guide for fixing the education systems of other countries. All countries are different, and as many Americans point out, Finland is a small nation with a much more homogeneous population than the United States.

Yet Sahlberg doesn't think that questions of size or homogeneity should give Americans reason to dismiss the Finnish example. Finland *is* a relatively homogeneous country—as of 2010, just 4.6 percent of Finnish residents had been born in another country, compared with 12.7 percent in the United States. But the number of foreign-born residents in Finland doubled during the decade leading up to 2010, and the country didn't lose its edge in education. Immigrants tended to concentrate in certain areas, causing some schools to become much more mixed than others, yet there has not been much change in the remarkable lack of variation between Finnish schools in the PISA surveys across the same period.

Samuel Abrams, a visiting scholar at Columbia University's Teachers College, has addressed the effects of size and homogeneity on a nation's education performance by comparing Finland with another Nordic country: Norway. Like Finland, Norway is small and not especially diverse overall, but unlike Finland it has taken an approach to education that is more American than Finnish. The result? Mediocre performance in the PISA survey. Educational policy, Abrams suggests, is probably more important to the success of a country's school system than the nation's size or ethnic makeup.

Indeed, Finland's population of 5.4 million can be compared to many an American state—after all, most American education is managed at the state level. According to the Migration Policy Institute, a research organization in Washington, there were 18 states in the U.S. in 2010 with an identical or significantly smaller percentage of foreign-born residents than Finland.

What's more, despite their many differences, Finland and the U.S. have an educational goal in common. When Finnish policymakers decided to reform the country's education system in the 1970s, they did so because they realized that to be competitive, Finland couldn't rely on manufacturing or its scant natural resources and instead had to invest in a knowledge-based economy.

With America's manufacturing industries now in decline, the goal of educational policy in the U.S.—as articulated by most everyone from President Obama on down—is to preserve American competitiveness by doing the same thing. Finland's experience suggests that to win at that game, a country has to prepare not just some of its population well, but all of its population well, for the new economy. To possess some of the best schools in the world might still not be good enough if there are children being left behind.

Is that an impossible goal? Sahlberg says that while his book isn't meant to be a how-to manual, it is meant to be a "pamphlet of hope."

"When President Kennedy was making his appeal for advancing American science and technology by putting a man on the moon by the end of the 1960s, many said it couldn't be done," Sahlberg said during his visit to New York. "But he had a dream. Just like Martin Luther King a few years later had a dream. Those dreams came true. Finland's dream was that we want to have a good public education for every child regardless of where they go to school or what kind of families they come from, and many even in Finland said it couldn't be done."

Clearly, many were wrong. It is possible to create equality. And perhaps even more important—as a challenge to the American way of thinking about education reform—Finland's experience shows that it is possible to achieve excellence by focusing not on competition, but on cooperation, and not on choice, but on equity.

The problem facing education in America isn't the ethnic diversity of the population but the economic inequality of society, and this is precisely the problem that Finnish education reform addressed. More equity at home might just be what America needs to be more competitive abroad.

1. How do cultural ideologies inform our attitudes about the aims of education?

2. How do current models of accountability in education in the U.S. reflect Western values?

3. How is "quality" defined in education in the United States? In other countries/cultures?

4. Is competition the best motivator in educational programs?

Kevin Slaten is program coordinator at China Labor Watch. In 2012, he completed a master's thesis on Chinese labor rights at Ohio State University. He also worked as an intern at New Urban Home in Qingdao, China, in 2012; he received a Fulbright Grant to study in Taiwan in 2009; and he was a Junior Fellow at the Carnegie Endowment for International Peace in 2008. He has written for publications such as Foreign Policy, South China Morning Post, and The Diplomat. Xue Chao was the program director for five years at New Urban Home, a labor NGO in Qingdao, China. He is currently studying law and plans to become a labor lawyer.

WAGES RISING IN CHINESE FACTORIES? ONLY FOR SOME

By Kevin Slaten and Xue Chao

If we are to take recent news reports at face value, the collective conscience of the world's consumers can be eased, because conditions at Chinese factories are improving.

Last year, *The New York Times* told us that these workers are "cheap no more," and just this February, the Heritage Foundation, touting the virtues of global free trade, claimed that Chinese factory wages have risen 20 percent per year since 2005. Foxconn, Apple's major supplier and the manufacturer of approximately 40 percent of the world's consumer electronics, says it will hold free union elections every five years.

But Pollyannas should take pause: The average migrant worker's $320 monthly salary in 2011 was actually 43 percent less than the $560 national average, according to government statistics. And though it's true that Foxconn will permit the election of union leaders, we have yet to see how much China's so-called democratic unions can empower the workers they purport to represent.

Skepticism and caveats aside, the reality is that the lot of formal production workers in China is indeed advancing, however slowly and painfully. But that is true only for *formal* workers. What many consumers and observers fail to note are the perilous conditions of

China's *temporary* production workers and the increased tendency among Chinese factories to use such workers to manufacture the brand-name products that fill your home.

Factories supplying Apple and Samsung, for example, make heavy use of temp workers. According to official statistics, temp workers make up 20 percent of China's urban workforce of 300 million, though the proportion in individual factories often tops 50 percent. As China turns into a land of short-term workers, there are grave implications for labor, companies, and Chinese society.

WHAT IS A CHINESE TEMP WORKER?

The two most common Chinese terms for temp workers are *linshigong* (临时工), literally "short-term workers," and *paiqiangong* (派遣工), "dispatch workers."

The second term is instructive. Temp workers in China are primarily recruited and assigned via *laowu paiqian gongsi* (劳务派遣公司), "labor dispatch companies." These are conceptually similar to America's staffing agencies.

Another thing Chinese and American temp workers share is a lack of benefits. Temp workers in a Chinese factory do not receive any type of insurance from the factories, leaving them with neither a health care safety net beneath them nor a retirement net ahead.

But working *sans* benefits is one of the few things all that American and Chinese temp workers have in common. While an American temp may be employed only 30 hours per week, a Chinese dispatch worker might spend 12 hours per day in a factory six or seven days a week.

What makes Chinese temp workers both unique and their plight urgent is the illegality of their conditions. Article 68 of Chinese labor law defines non-full-time workers as those employed no more than 24 hours per week and an average of four hours per day, filling a company's short-term temporary needs. But the reality is that such workers do more overtime than the law permits, lack a contractual relationship with their employers, and are often paid sub-minimum wages.

Labor dispatch companies are also often the channel through which child workers—under the age of 16 in China—end up in factories. Dispatch companies charge workers $50 to $100 in service fees, so to the company a child worker is simply another source of revenue.

WHY DO TEMP WORKERS EXIST?

Businesses gain considerable cost-saving benefits by using temp workers in their factories. Temp workers do not sign a contract with the factories, relieving the company of responsibility for providing these workers with the five types of insurance mandated by Chinese law. In a mid-sized factory with 500 temp workers, the company could save tens of thousands of dollars per month in insurance payments alone.

Another long-term benefit for companies is that they do not have to employ veteran workers who might require higher pay. Rather, the company can let temp workers come and go, then hire the next batch of cheap young temps. In cases where workers are injured, the company is less likely to be forced to pay compensation because the worker does not have evidence of a contractual relationship. Finally, factories can skimp on making their facilities more pleasing for workers since the workers are not expected to stay.

Temp workers do gain some benefits, however short-sighted they may be. Using the temp route, workers have a sense of freedom. Factories make promises during recruiting that end up being distant from the true working and living conditions within, and managers are often unkind or condescending toward workers, most of whom have less than a high school education. For these reasons, workers may understandably wish to avoid dealing with the stresses of being a formal employee in the factory. The thinking is, "If the supervisor has it in for me, I can simply leave and get assigned elsewhere."

Another reason one may prefer to be a temp worker is the frequency of pay. In China, where factory profit margins are often thin, employees commonly get stuck working without pay. Temp workers can sometimes avoid the wage-arrears headache when they get paid daily or weekly.

Poor governance in China has played a major role in the rise of the temp phenomenon. The text of Chinese law is generally pro-labor. But in reality, collusion between local government and business interests—and the oiled gears of bribery—have led to severely sub-par law enforcement.

THE RISKS OF A TEMP WORKER EMPIRE

The most apparent victims of an economy that relies on temp workers are, of course, the workers themselves. The price they pay for the freedom to walk away is unequal treatment under law, a lack of economic security, and a weakened ability to defend their rights. Unlike formal employees, temp workers are often paid less and do not usually receive insurance. If they are injured on the job, they must depend on their own meager savings, those of their economically disadvantaged families, or the benevolence of the factory. If a worker wants to take a job-injury or rights-violation case to court, her legal standing is diminished because she lacks a contract with her employer.

The system also presents risks to business. First and foremost, the conduct surrounding the employment of temp workers is illegal in China, and businesses risk being sued or criminally indicted for their behavior. Economically, while the up-front savings for a company may seem obvious, temp workers will be unfamiliar with the production process and less committed to the factory; the result is inefficiency and a greater number of deficient products.

At a broader political level, with intermittent work and illegally unequal wages, the growing temp worker population contradicts the Chinese government's professed commitment to reducing economic inequality (Chinese). On the government's priority list, social stability comes a close second to development, and the growth of a transient, marginalized social group is not conducive to stability.

TURNING BACK THE TIDE OF TEMPS

When the numbers are crunched, businesses using temps can perhaps improve their bottom lines. But this wanton pursuit of profit is illegal, unethical, and a poor standardization of business practices. Chinese factories and the global brands they supply have a social responsibility to respect the value of full-time jobs and eradicate the illegal use of temp workers.

Workers and labor-rights NGOs, for their part, must continue to increase awareness among the worker community of the risks of temp work and the rights of labor.

The Chinese government has an obvious responsibility to strengthen the enforcement of its own laws. Indeed, in December the government strengthened restrictions on the use of temp workers, but without effective enforcement, these are empty expressions and may only serve to further diminish the respect for law.

Lastly, the duty of foreign governments is clear: The U.N. Guiding Principles on Business and Human Rights, unanimously endorsed by developed countries, states that a government has the duty to prevent companies operating in its jurisdiction from violating laws and impinging on human rights in other jurisdictions. The U.S. and others should pass national laws that punish companies for labor violations in foreign territories. Such a law would have the support of Americans, who know that "injustice anywhere is a threat to justice everywhere."

1. The authors state, "Workers and labor-rights NGOs, for their part, must continue to increase awareness among the worker community of the risks of temp work and the rights of labor." What exactly are the risks of temp workers as outlined in the article? Why might workers prefer temp positions?

2. As one of their solutions, the authors write, "The U.S. and others should pass national laws that punish companies for labor violations in foreign territories." What implications could this have on our consumer industry or foreign relations? Remember that the article notes, "Factories supplying Apple and Samsung, for example, make heavy use of temp workers." Do you support this idea? Why or why not?

PERSPECTIVE

Natasha Trethewey is the Robert W. Woodruff Professor of English and Creative Writing at Emory University, where she also directs the Creative Writing Program. She won the 2007 Pulitzer Prize in Poetry for her 2006 collection Native Guard *and was appointed United States Poet Laureate in June 2012.*

ON WHITMAN, CIVIL WAR MEMORY, AND MY SOUTH

By Natasha Trethewey

O magnet-South! O glistening perfumed South! my South!
O quick mettle, rich blood, impulse and love! good and evil!
O all dear to me!

—Walt Whitman

I. THE NEW SOUTH

A few years ago I was interviewed for the *Atlanta Journal-Constitution*—a newspaper whose slogan used to be "Covering Dixie Like the Dew"—and later, when the article appeared, the headline read, "Poet Digs at Secrets in Her South." Not long after that, I received several e-mail and phone messages from a marketing representative who wanted to get a few lines from me about "my South." In the messages, he said it wouldn't take long and that his firm couldn't pay me for my comments. Well, I was busy, and besides that, I figured he didn't want to hear what I really think about the South. Most likely, he probably wanted some sound-bite clichés about how I like my grits, sweet tea, or barbecue, about how we southerners like sitting on porches and after-church visiting.

Some time after that, I started seeing advertisements for Turner South Network on the sides of buses all around Atlanta. Usually the ads featured a photograph of a man or woman next to a quote about his or her South. The text suggested the kinds of things I suspect that marketing representative was looking for when he tried to contact me; and though I don't know whether it had been the network calling me or not, I couldn't help thinking that there might be some connection. Not only were these images of the New South appearing on buses, they were showing up in some clever and entertaining television commercials too.

In one commercial, a long-haired teenager is driving fast down a dusty road—until he gets pulled over by a police officer. The officer appears menacing behind his metallic aviator sunglasses, and he has the kind of belly and demeanor that are reminiscent of some country sheriff straight out of Hazzard County. Approaching the car, the police officer stands—almost threateningly—for a moment, then says, lifting his shades, "Son, don't forget to pick your sister up from ballet." This is the new South—a riff on the stereotypes of the not-so-new South—and the message is certainly one of change. It's a comforting thought—if not completely true. Watching it, I thought of Walt Whitman and his South: how even his love for this place is underscored by something we'll never see in these commercials or on buses rolling through Atlanta.

The South of Whitman's time was not without its stunning beauty or its stunning cruelty. Writing "O Magnet South" in 1860, Whitman praised the landscape—its rivers, lakes, trees, the native flora and fauna:

> O the cotton plant! The growing fields of rice, sugar, hemp!
>
> The cactus guarded with thorns, the laurel tree with large white flowers . . .

His love for the South, however, was complex, and in the poem he acknowledges, too, the darker side of it—"the piney odor and the gloom, the awful natural stillness." When he goes further to mention "the fugitive" and his "conceal'd hut," it is hard not to think of fugitive slaves. Whitman's take on the South is much like my own; it is a love/hate relationship. Later, he would write: "I would be the last one to confuse moral values—to imagine the South impeccable. I don't condone the South where it has gone wrong—its Negro slavery, I don't condone that—far from it—I hate it." Because of his open-armed enthusiasm, his inclusiveness and celebration of everyone, even the lowliest prostitute or degraded slave, Whitman's work has come to represent a poetics of democracy, a humane tradition of antiracism. Even now, there is much more to be learned from him and from his conflicted relationship to his subject matter—especially as Americans near and far are still fighting, ideologically, the Civil War.

II. THE LOST WAR

E. O. Wilson has written, "Homo Sapiens is the only species to suffer psychological exile." I've been thinking about that a lot lately, particularly in relation to all the panels I have been on at conferences on contemporary southern literature and culture. I began to notice, after several of these panels, that someone in the audience almost always raised a question about the psyches of southern writers—why we write the way that we do. It seemed to me that just as often, someone on the panel would answer that question by saying something like, "We southerners write the way that we do because, after all, we lost the war." Each time I've heard this I've had to say, "My South didn't lose the war." On each of these occasions, the other panelists—most likely unintentionally—had responded to the question in a manner that seemed to suggest they had forgotten I was there, and that seemed to define the southern psyche and the southern experience as if they were monolithic. In a sense, their responses echo a type of erasure that has affected the documenting of public history and the dedication of public monuments and has continued to affect our public memory. I'm sure my fellow panelists never meant to exclude me when they said "we." I am a southerner too, but these occurrences are evidence of the public memory of the war and its aftermath that still makes outsiders of black Americans—even as nearly 200,000 fought for freedom in the Civil War—and leaves out many narratives which would give us a fuller, richer understanding of our American experience.

A champion of American experience—the diversity of its people and their labors—Whitman feared that the "real war" would not get written. He believed that war existed in the alternative narrative that might be offered by so many anonymous soldiers—most dead and buried, often in unmarked graves—whose stories would never be told. Whitman's Specimen Days becomes a kind of monument to the common soldier—

the harsh facts of war recorded in his honest language. And yet, there is still little written of black soldiers, though he mentions tending to them as well: "Among the black soldiers, wounded or sick, and in the contraband camps, I also took my way whenever in their neighborhood, and did what I could for them." This is only a slight acknowledgment from the poet who wrote with great inclusiveness of blacks in such poems as "I Sing the Body Electric" and "Song of Myself." Perhaps a more telling poem, however—one that suggests the complexity of Whitman's conflicted relationship to the South and all her citizens—is "Reconciliation."

> Word over all, beautiful as the sky!
>
> Beautiful that war, and all its deeds of carnage, must in time be utterly lost;
>
> That the hands of the sisters Death and Night incessantly Softly wash again, and ever again, this soil'd world;
>
> . . . For my enemy is dead, a man divine as myself is dead;
>
> I look where he lies white-faced and still in the coffin—I draw near;
>
> Bend down and touch lightly with my lips the white face in the coffin.

Here, Whitman suggests the reunion of the nation, men on opposite sides of the war drawn together beneath the banner of reconciliation. However, in the final image of the dead, "white-faced" in the coffin, Whitman leaves out the reality of so many dead soldiers whose faces were not white. And further, according to historian David Blight, the poem highlights—in the "kinship" of the dead white brothers—"the ultimate betrayal of the dark-faced folk whom the dead had shared in liberating." This kind of erasure would continue to dominate Civil War memory as monuments to only part of the story inscribed a narrative on the American landscape—particularly in the South. The lost war, then, is the narrative of black Americans whose stories were often subjugated, lost, or left out of public memory and the creation of public monuments.

III. MEMORY AND FORGETTING

Just off the coast of my hometown, Gulfport, Mississippi, is a series of barrier islands—Cat, Horn, Deer, and Ship—that separate the dirty waters of the coastal area, with its dead fish and debris, from the clearer waters out in the Gulf. Ship Island is a Civil War site, and during the warmer months, anyone can buy passage on one of the small cruisers making daily trips out there and take a brief tour offered by the National Park Service.

The island's history is an interesting one. The first regiments of the Louisiana Native Guards were mustered into service in September, October, and November of 1862—the 1st regiment thus becoming the first officially sanctioned regiment of black soldiers in the Union Army, and the 2nd and 3rd made up of men who had been slaves only months before enlisting. During the war, the fort at Ship Island, Mississippi, called Fort Massachusetts, was maintained as a prison for Confederate soldiers—military convicts and prisoners of war—manned by the 2nd regiment. In his wartime reminiscences, Whitman pointed out that "few white regiments [made] a better appearance on parade than the 1st and 2nd Louisiana Native Guards." And yet, visitors to the fort today will learn almost none of this history. Instead, they will see first the plaque placed at the entrance by the Daughters of the Confederacy listing the names of the Confederate men once there. Nowhere is a similar plaque memorializing the names of the Native Guards, and if tourists don't know to ask about the history of these black soldiers, most likely the park ranger will overlook this aspect of the fort's history in his tour, mentioning only that this was a fort taken over by Union forces and that Confederate prisoners were kept there. Even the brochures leave out any mention that the troops stationed on the island were black. This omission serves to further the narrative that blacks were passive recipients of the freedom bestowed upon them by white "brothers" who fought and died in the Civil War.

Monuments all around the South serve to inscribe a particular narrative onto the landscape while at the same time subjugating or erasing another. Fortunately, there are several organizations and historians trying to restore the history of the role of black soldiers to the public memory through monuments. Last February, in the Vicksburg

National Military Park, the first monument of its kind in a national park was erected, though not without certain omissions. According to the Jackson Advocate, during the earlier ground-breaking ceremony, "Park Superintendent Bill Nichols and Park historian Terry Winschel begrudgingly labeled the black regiments as 'supply guards' in the text on display rather than giving the men their full measure of respect as the fully-recognized infantry, artillery and cavalry units that they were."

That a more inclusive history of black soldiers is not given on Ship Island or in the Vicksburg Military Park, and that certain facts are often left out of local historical narratives and (perhaps until most recently) were likely to be given only a small part in larger histories, is emblematic of ideological contests about how to remember the Civil War, how we construct public memory with its omissions and embellishments. As David Blight asserts in *Race and Reunion: The Civil War in American Memory*, "Deflections and evasions, careful remembering and necessary forgetting, and embittered and irreconcilable versions of experience are all the stuff of historical memory." Though Whitman had acknowledged black soldiers in his letters and reminiscences, ultimately he often left blacks out of his larger concerns: "When the South is spoken of," he wrote, contrasting the roles of the ruling class and the masses, "no one means the people, the mass of freemen." Here Whitman is referring to the free white masses, even as his language reminds us of the invisible "freedmen" all around the South. In fact, according to Daniel Aaron in The Unwritten War:

> the Negro did not figure significantly in his calculations for America's future, the Grand Plan of History; and it is just as mistaken to confuse Whitman's prose opinion of the Negro and the poetic use he made of him in "Leaves of Grass" as it is to identify his antislavery position with abolitionism.

At the ground-breaking ceremony for the new monument, historian Jim Woodrich's words seemed to echo Whitman's more-than-a-century-old prediction that the real war would not get into the books: "By being here today," Woodrich began, "we acknowledge the valor and honor" of the black Union troops. Their story, he said, "yearns to be known."

IV. "THE REAL WAR WILL NOT GET INTO THE BOOKS"

William Faulkner has said, "the past isn't dead; it isn't even past." All around us debates about the memory of the Civil War and its aftermath continue to shape contemporary concerns. In many states, the battle over the meaning of the Confederate flag is ongoing, with revisionist versions abounding. Here in Georgia, the battle connects us not only to the Civil War but also to public opposition to desegregation. In Mississippi, my home state, the flag still flies on the beach between Gulfport and Biloxi as a monument to only part of our shared history, whereas an equally significant history is overlooked—that of other southerners, black former slaves who were stationed at Ship Island and who fought for their own freedom and citizenship in contests not far away, thus helping the nation come a bit closer to realizing the full democratic potential outlined in the Constitution. These issues are, ultimately, fights about remembrance—how we see ourselves as Americans within the context of history.

When the Daughters of the Confederacy mounted the plaque at Ship Island, they were working to inscribe their exclusive version of history into the public memory, leaving out the other population on the island. C. Vann Woodward, in his preface to *Jumpin' Jim Crow: Southern Politics from Civil War to Civil Rights*, asserts that during the last two decades of the 19th century and the first two of the 20th it was "white ladies . . . who bore primary responsibility for the myths glorifying the old order, the Lost Cause, and white supremacy." Woodward is referring, specifically, to the United Daughters of the Confederacy, the Daughters of the American Revolution, Daughters of Pilgrims, and Daughters of Colonial Governors; they were considered "guardians of the past." "Non-daughters," he writes, "were excluded." The efforts of the Daughters of the Confederacy extended beyond the erecting of monuments and the naming of roads; indeed, they commissioned the history textbooks written for southern schools and oversaw the material contained within them in order to control the narrative of the South's role in the war—that is, to tell a story that was rife with omissions and embellishments, that sought to cast the causes of the war only in terms of states' rights and not at all in terms of the matter of slavery.

It would seem that Whitman, in his conflicted attitudes toward the roles of both North and South, toward slavery and black suffrage (he hated slavery but did not believe blacks capable of exercising the vote), could foresee such one-sided narratives and the need for a fuller understanding of the roots of the conflict—a history more inclusive than what would be told and written for several generations: "But what of the main premonitions of the war?" he asked. Decades later, W. E. B. DuBois would begin to answer him—furthering Whitman's own ideas about the war's origins—and in so doing, point out the embellishments and omissions in the history put forth by a generation of scholars. In his essay "The Propaganda of History," DuBois would take to task American historians, asserting that among the profession, "we have too often made a deliberate attempt so to change the facts of history that the story will make pleasant reading for Americans."

Whitman knew all too well that the real war he feared would not get written was not a pleasant one. Referring primarily to the "seething hell and the black infernal background of countless minor scenes," he nonetheless foreshadows another backdrop—the narratives of blacks relegated to the margins of public memory. "Long, long hence," he anticipated, "when the grave has quenched many hot prejudices and vitalities, and an entirely new class of thinkers and writers come to the argument, the complete question, can perhaps be fairly weighed."

V. WHAT WOULD WHITMAN DO?

On billboards around the South and on church marquees proclaiming the theme of upcoming sermons, a frequent question stands out: What Would Jesus Do? I ask, instead, what would our earthly father—father of modern American poetry, father of the poetry of a democratic vision—what would our Whitman do? OK, so this question is overly speculative. I can hear the voices out there saying that people are products of their historical moment. The defenders of Thomas Jefferson as well as his detractors are getting their guard up. I'm not interested in arguing the omissions of the past, only the restoration of those omissions in the present. Perhaps not restoration: acknowledgment is a better word. When Robert Penn Warren returned to his South to write *Segregation*, he was a man in the midst of change—he was rethinking his position as a contributor to the anthology *I'll Take My Stand*. The nation was changing, and he was changing along with it.

When Whitman took on the task of setting down on paper some of his thoughts about the Civil War, its causes and its aftermath, he probably did not have the image of the black soldier in the foreground of his thinking. Though his wartime reminiscences would consider regiments of black troops, his poem "Ethiopia Saluting the Colors" focuses on a "dusky woman, so ancient hardly human," and not black soldiers who were participants in the war rather than bystanders. However, the omissions, inherent even in his later writings about the war, underscore the questions of historical memory with which future generations would contend:

> Probably no future age can know, but I well know, how the gist of this fiercest and most resolute of the world's warlike contentions resided exclusively in the unnamed, unknown rank and file; and how the brunt of its labor of death was, to all essential purposes, volunteered.

Here, Whitman directs us to the unnamed, unknown rank-and-file white soldier and, inadvertently, to black soldiers as well—the legions of runaway slaves and freedmen who flocked to Union camps, first as contraband and then later as men (and women) eager to enlist—whose story has been left out of public memory of the Civil War and has only begun to be inscribed onto the man-made, monumental American landscape.

VI. CODA

A lot of things have changed since Whitman declared his love for the South and her contradictions. Some have not. Contradictions abound in this landscape of beauty and ugliness, this cauldron of nostalgic remembrances and willed forgetting. In Mississippi and Alabama, lawyers and concerned citizens are continuing to work to bring to trial the perpetrators of heinous crimes—Byron de la Beckwith; the bombers who blew up a church in Birmingham, killing four little girls; the men responsible for the murders of Cheney, Schwerner, and Goodman. An exhibit about the history of lynching is touring the country, even as opponents of this necessary remembering here in Atlanta opine in letters to the editor that some things are best left buried, forgotten. I live with the ghosts of the past every day; when Halloween comes around, I see in the decorative skeletons hanging from my neighbors' trees the specter of lynching. And even worse, I encounter the specter of what put real bodies in trees still lingering in the kind of willed forgetting and intolerance we haven't yet overcome. From where I stand, it's easy to feel the kind of contradictions evident in Whitman's work, those things he revealed both intentionally and inadvertently.

Like him, I love my South. And I hate it too.

1. Trethewey writes about the way society views the past. What role does memory play in the perception of history in the United States?

2. Trethewey discusses different historical perspectives of the South. Consider the region where you or your family grew up, and list some notable historical events associated with that region. Then write about how memory and what is recorded in history might have affected the region's historical identity. Can you identify any possible gaps in history?

Thomas Rogers is a translator currently living in Berlin. He is a freelance journalist with Slate, was the former editor of Salon, and has also contributed to NY Mag, TNR, and The Awl. Slate is a United-States-based English language online current affairs and culture magazine. Slate is a division of the Washington Post Company.

FOR HELP IN OLD AGE, HOW ABOUT A NEW AGE OF ROBOTS?

By Thomas Rogers

Early in the new science-fiction film *Robot & Frank*, Frank, an elderly man, gets a visit from his son, Hunter. Worried about his father's apparent decline, Hunter takes a gift out of the back of his car: a white robot with a humanlike body and a polite speaking voice. The machine, Hunter promises, will keep his dad healthy and focused—and the house clean. Frank is not so sure, though: "That thing's going to kill me in my sleep," he worries.

But before long, the "health care" robot is cooking his meals, planting a garden and planning activities to keep his human overlord occupied.

The film's depiction of robot-human relations may still be a fantasy, but it's also a reminder we've been expecting elder care robots like Frank's in the real world for several years now, and so far, they're nowhere to be seen. So what's the hold-up?

It's no secret that America is getting older. By 2030, thanks to the baby boomers, one in five Americans will be 65 or older, stressing the health care system and economy. Half of those over 85 require assistance in everyday activities, and, if 2009 numbers hold up, more than 13 percent of people over 85 will spend time in nursing homes. It's unclear who will pay for this and how. And more importantly, it's unclear who will take care of all of these old people.

The solution, the robotics industry hopes, is technology. In Japan, where panic over an aging population is nothing new, elder care robots have been a priority for more than a decade. One of the Japanese researchers' bigger successes is Paro, a touch-sensitive companion robot—a sort of high-tech stuffed animal, shaped like a seal—for elderly people with cognitive disorders like Alzheimer's. Japanese Nursebots can lift up elderly patients and bring them breakfast in bed, and this year, researchers from Japan's Chukyo University released Babyloid, a baby-like robot similar to Paro that looks like something that crawled out of a Miyazaki movie.

In recent years, Japanese tech giant Panasonic has created a hair-washing robot, a drug delivery robot, a robotic bed, and HOSPI-Rimo, a robot with a touchscreen that helps hospital patients communicate with doctors and family.

In the next decade, the selection of personal elder care robots is expected to expand dramatically in the United States as well. "Full robots with arms are still very expensive," says Ashutosh Saxena, a professor in the department of computer science at Cornell, "but they are getting cheaper by the day."

He predicts that armless robots—capable of communicating verbally with the elderly and observing them in case of accidents—will hit the market within the next five years. These kinds of robots, which could even monitor a person's medication intake, should allow elderly people to live independently and healthily longer, like a very sophisticated Life Alert bracelet.

There's just one hiccup: the elderly themselves.

Despite manufacturers' hopes, robotic technology has proven to be alienating for many older people—even, the BBC reports, in Japan, a country with an intense, long-term love of all things robotic. Alexander Libin, scientific director of simulation and education research at Medstar Health Research Institute, argues that one of the biggest challenges is that the elderly need to be able to communicate easily with them. Although many robots (and mobile phones) can now recognize voice commands, nonverbal cues pose a much bigger challenge. Libin, who has worked extensively on robot-patient interaction, believes that touch-sensitive technology—like the one used by Paro, the therapeutic seal robot—will play a large role in making robots palatable to seniors. DARPA, the government-funded research institute, is working on neural robot limb communication, a technology that, Libin believes, could be applied to robots.

Given the elderly population's diverse needs, elder care robots will also likely be far more specialized than *Robot & Frank's* robotic helper suggests. "People with chronic illnesses like diabetes need a robot that can help them with shots, people with bad vision need guidance, people with cancer that are in pain will need a robot to entertain them by having a conversation or reading a book," says Libin. The coming generation of robots, he says, will be created with those specific goals in mind.

Unlike the Japanese, American engineers have been focusing on robots that are more practical and less humanoid. "The Japanese want robots to be like them," says Libin, noting Japan's long tradition of treating inanimate objects like living beings. In the United States, we're more comfortable treating machines as machines. "We want things we can control."

The path toward robot acceptance may also require something very simple and, for robot manufacturers, frustrating: patience. The process of getting old people to be comfortable with robots, Saxena argues, will be a question of gradual acclimatization. Elderly people will have to get used to having small, nonthreatening observer robots watching them in their homes before they'll allow robots do tasks on their behalf—or even touch them.

And the truth is, boomers who grew up long before the rise of computers or smartphones may never be comfortable with the idea of replacing a human being with a machine. Like other forms of social change, robot acceptance may simply require one generation to replace the previous one.

Robots can be a technology that is difficult for the elderly to accept. Apart from the technology, what are some of the human relationship challenges associated with the elderly relying on robotic assistance? Is there a limit to their effectiveness? Is there a trade-off between independence and isolation when the elderly rely on robots?

Judy Lin is a writer with the UCLA Today news site www.today.ucla.edu. She has also freelanced for Prevention magazine and other publications.

HONOR OR ABANDON: SOCIETIES' TREATMENT OF ELDERLY INTRIGUES SCHOLAR

BY JUDY LIN

When people grow old in traditional villages in Fiji, family and friends care for them at home until their dying days. In America, the elderly are more typically sent to nursing homes—a contrast that may appear unfeeling, even cruel. But the ways in which societies around the world treat their elderly span a vast and varied range, according to Jared Diamond, UCLA professor of geography and physiology.

Why this differs so drastically from culture to culture is an intriguing question that Diamond, 72, a Pulitzer Prize-winning author of *Guns, Germs, and Steel: The Fates of Human Societies* and recipient of a MacArthur Foundation "genius" award, is currently researching. Recently, he shared some of his thoughts on the subject with a standing-room-only audience in the Neuroscience Research Building auditorium in a lecture, "Honor or Abandon: Why Does Treatment of the Elderly Vary so Widely Among Human Societies?"

The idea that it's human nature for parents to make sacrifices for their children and, in turn, for their grown children to sacrifice for their aging parents—turns out to be a "naïve expectation," said Diamond. This assumption, he said, ignores undeniable conflicts of interest between generations.

From a common sense perspective, "Parents and children both want a comfortable life—there are limits to the sacrifices that they'll make for each other." And from a scientific perspective—natural selection—Diamond noted, "It may under some circumstances be better for children to abandon or kill their parents and for the parents to abandon or kill their children."

Those circumstances include life's often heart-wrenching realities—from the threat of starvation among indigenous tribes to the difficult choices posed by modern societies' life-prolonging medical care, Diamond said.

Traditional nomadic tribes often end up abandoning their elderly during their unrelenting travels. The choice for the healthy and young is to do this or carry the old and infirm on their backs—along with children, weapons and necessities—through perilous territory. Also prone to sacrificing their elderly are societies that suffer periodic famines. Citing a dramatic example, Diamond said Paraguay's Aché Indians assign certain young men the task of killing old people with an ax or spear, or burying them alive.

"We react with horror at these stories, but upon reflection, what else could they do?" Diamond asked. "The people in these societies are faced with a cruel choice."

Those of us in modern cultures face cruel choices of our own, he added. "Many of you have already faced or will face a similar ordeal when you are the relative responsible for the medical care of an old person—the one who has to decide whether to halt further medical intervention or whether to administer painkillers and sedatives that will have the side effect of hastening death."

Yet the fact remains, Diamond said, that many societies treat their elderly better than Americans do. In some cultures, he said, children are so devoted that when their aging parents lose their teeth the children will pre-chew their food. A closer look at how traditional societies value (or don't value) their old people might teach us what to emulate and what to avoid.

The elderly's usefulness in a society plays a big part in determining their fate, Diamond said. While old people in traditional societies can no longer spear game or battle enemies, they can still gather food to care for children. They are also often expert at making tools, weapons, baskets and clothes. In many societies they serve as "tribal elders" in medicine, religion and politics.

Perhaps most important, in cultures lacking written records of history, song and other forms of culture, older people are invaluable sources of information.

"The repositories of knowledge are the memories of old people," Diamond said. "If you don't have old people to remember what happened 50 years ago, you've lost a lot of experience for that society," from communal history to advice on how to survive a cyclone or other natural disaster.

Societies also vary in how much they respect their old people—or don't. In East Asian cultures steeped in a Confucian tradition that places a high value on filial piety, obedience and respect, Diamond said, "it is considered utterly despicable not to take care of your elderly parents." The same goes for Mediterranean cultures, where multigenerational families live together in the same house—in stark contrast to the United States, "where routinely, old people do not live with their children and it's a big hassle to take care of your parents even if you want to do it."

While modernization has brought many benefits to the elderly—most notably improved health and longer life spans—it has also led to a breakdown of traditions. For example, multigenerational families are becoming a thing of the past in many modern cities in China, Japan and India, Diamond said, where "today's young people want privacy, want to go off and have a home of their own."

In America, Diamond said, a "cult of youth" and emphasis on the virtues of independence, individualism and self-reliance also make life hard on older people as they inevitably lose some of these traits. Then, there's America's Protestant work ethic, "which holds that if you're no longer working, you've lost the main value that society places on you." Retirement also means losing social relationships, which, coupled with

America's high mobility, leaves many old people hundreds or even thousands of miles away from longtime friends and family.

Modern literacy and its ties to technology are also putting the elderly at a disadvantage.

"Modern literacy means that we look up things in books or on the Internet—we don't go ask an old person," Diamond said. "Formal educational systems, such as UCLA, replace old people with highly trained professors for transmitting specialized knowledge."

And lightning-speed technological advances "mean that the things that old people do understand got technologically outdated," Diamond said, adding that his ability to multiply two-digit numbers in his head has now been superseded by pocket calculators. He even admitted to having to consult his teenage sons to use the TV's "remote with 47 buttons on it."

Still, steps can be taken to improve the lives of our elderly, Diamond said. Understand their changing strengths and weaknesses as they age, he advised, and appreciate their deeper understanding of human relationships and their ability to think across wide-ranging disciplines, to strategize, and share what they've learned.

"So if you want to get advice on complicated problems, ask someone who's 70; don't ask someone who's 25," Diamond concluded. "Old people can have new value ... although we often don't recognize that this is possible."

1. Do some research to find out how the elderly are treated in different countries around the world. Reflect on your reaction by considering your cultural norms and how they differ from the culture you've studied.

2. "Virtues of independence, individualism and self-reliance" are highly valued in the United States. Reflect on highly valued character traits in your culture or sub-culture and how they have affected your treatment of the elderly.

Gene Luen Yang is a Chinese American writer who currently teaches at Hamline University in Minnesota. He is a well-known voice in comics and literature, having published work with Marvel, Dark Horse, and Harper Collins. In 2007, Yang's book American Born Chinese *became the first graphic novel to win the Michael L. Printz Award.*

AMERICAN BORN CHINESE

BY GENE LUEN YANG

1. What are some of the misconceptions about different groups living in the United States? Why do people have these ideas?

2. What is the significance of the school Jin attends being called Mayflower Elementary?

Elizabeth Kolbert was a writer for the New York Times *from 1984 to 1999 and has been writing for* The New Yorker *ever since. She grew up in New York, attended Yale University, and received the Fulbright Scholarship to study at the Universität Hamburg, in Germany. Her book about global warming,* Field Notes from a Catastrophe, *won the 2006 National Magazine Award for Public Interest, the 2006 National Academies Communication Award, and the 2005 American Association for the Advancement of Science Journalism Award. She now resides in Massachusetts with her family.*

SPOILED ROTTEN: WHY DO KIDS RULE THE ROOST?

By Elizabeth Kolbert

In 2004, Carolina Izquierdo, an anthropologist at the University of California, Los Angeles, spent several months with the Matsigenka, a tribe of about twelve thousand people who live in the Peruvian Amazon. The Matsigenka hunt for monkeys and parrots, grow yucca and bananas, and build houses that they roof with the leaves of a particular kind of palm tree, known as a *kapashi*. At one point, Izquierdo decided to accompany a local family on a leaf-gathering expedition down the Urubamba River.

A member of another family, Yanira, asked if she could come along. Izquierdo and the others spent five days on the river. Although Yanira had no clear role in the group, she quickly found ways to make herself useful. Twice a day, she swept the sand off the sleeping mats, and she helped stack the *kapashi* leaves for transport back to the village. In the evening, she fished for crustaceans, which she cleaned, boiled, and served to the others. Calm and self-possessed, Yanira "asked for nothing," Izquierdo later recalled. The girl's behavior made a strong impression on the anthropologist because at the time of the trip Yanira was just six years old.

While Izquierdo was doing field work among the Matsigenka, she was also involved in an anthropological study closer to home. A colleague of hers, Elinor Ochs, had recruited thirty-two middle-class families for a study of life in twenty-first-century Los Angeles. Ochs had arranged to have the families filmed as they ate, fought, made up, and did the dishes.

Izquierdo and Ochs shared an interest in many ethnographic issues, including child rearing. How did parents in different cultures train young people to assume adult responsibilities? In the case of the Angelenos, they mostly didn't. In the L.A. families observed, no child routinely performed household chores without being instructed to. Often, the kids had to be begged to attempt the simplest tasks; often, they still refused. In one fairly typical encounter, a father asked his eight-year-old son five times to please go take a bath or a shower. After the fifth plea went unheeded, the father picked the boy up and carried him into the bathroom. A few minutes later, the kid, still unwashed, wandered into another room to play a video game.

In another representative encounter, an eight-year-old girl sat down at the dining table. Finding that no silverware had been laid out for her, she demanded, "How am I supposed to eat?" Although the girl clearly knew where the silverware was kept, her father got up to get it for her.

In a third episode captured on tape, a boy named Ben was supposed to leave the house with his parents. But he couldn't get his feet into his sneakers, because the laces were tied. He handed one of the shoes to his father: "Untie it!" His father suggested that he ask nicely.

"Can you untie it?" Ben replied. After more back-and-forth, his father untied Ben's sneakers. Ben put them on, then asked his father to retie them. "*You* tie your shoes and let's *go*," his father finally exploded. Ben was unfazed. "I'm just *asking*," he said.

A few years ago, Izquierdo and Ochs wrote an article for *Ethos*, the journal of the Society of Psychological Anthropology, in which they described Yanira's conduct during the trip down the river and Ben's exchange with his dad. "Juxtaposition of these developmental stories begs for an account of responsibility in childhood," they wrote. Why do Matsigenka children "help their families at home more than L.A. children?" And "Why do L.A. adult family members help their children at home more than do Matsigenka?" Though not phrased in exactly such terms, questions like these are being asked—silently, imploringly, despairingly—every single day by parents from Anchorage to Miami. Why, why, why?

With the exception of the imperial offspring of the Ming dynasty and the dauphins of pre-Revolutionary France, contemporary American kids may represent the most indulged young people in the history of the world. It's not just that they've been given unprecedented amounts of stuff—clothes, toys, cameras, skis, computers, televisions, cell phones, PlayStations, iPods. (The market for Burberry Baby and other forms of kiddie "couture" has reportedly been growing by ten percent a year.) They've also been granted unprecedented authority. "Parents want their kids' approval, a reversal of the past ideal of children striving for their parents' approval," Jean Twenge and W. Keith Campbell, both professors of psychology, have written. In many middle-class families, children have one, two, sometimes three adults at their beck and call. This is a social experiment on a grand scale, and a growing number of adults fear that it isn't working out so well: according to one poll, commissioned by *Time* and CNN, two-thirds of American parents think that their children are spoiled.

The notion that we may be raising a generation of kids who can't, or at least won't, tie their own shoes has given rise to a new genre of parenting books. Their titles tend to be either dolorous ("The Price of Privilege") or downright hostile ("The Narcissism Epidemic," "Mean Moms Rule," "A Nation of Wimps"). The books are less how-to guides than how-not-to's: how not to give in to your toddler, how not to intervene whenever your teenager looks bored, how not to spend two hundred thousand dollars on tuition only to find your twenty-something graduate back at home, drinking all your beer.

Not long ago, Sally Koslow, a former editor-in-chief of *McCall's*, discovered herself in this last situation. After four years in college and two on the West Coast, her son Jed moved back to Manhattan and settled into his old room in the family's apartment, together with thirty-four boxes of vinyl LPs. Unemployed, Jed liked to stay out late, sleep until noon, and wander around in his boxers. Koslow set out to try to understand why he and so many of his peers seemed stuck in what she regarded as permanent "adultescence." She concluded that one of the reasons is the lousy economy. Another is parents like her.

"Our offspring have simply leveraged our braggadocio, good intentions, and overinvestment," Koslow writes in her new book, *Slouching Toward Adulthood: Observations from the Not-So-Empty Nest* (Viking). They inhabit "a broad savannah of entitlement that we've watered, landscaped, and hired gardeners to maintain." She recommends letting the grasslands revert to forest: "The best way for a lot of us to show our love would be to learn to un-mother and un-father." One practical tip that she offers is to do nothing when your adult child finally decides to move out. In the process of schlepping Jed's stuff to an apartment in Carroll Gardens, Koslow's husband tore a tendon and ended up in emergency surgery.

Madeline Levine, a psychologist who lives outside San Francisco, specializes in treating young adults. In *Teach Your Children Well: Parenting for Authentic Success* (HarperCollins), she argues that we do too much for our kids because we overestimate our influence. "Never before have parents been so (mistakenly) convinced that their every move has a ripple effect into their child's future success," she writes. Paradoxically, Levine maintains, by working so hard to help our kids we end up holding them back.

"Most parents today were brought up in a culture that put a strong emphasis on being special," she observes. "Being special takes hard work and can't be trusted to children. Hence the exhausting cycle of constantly monitoring their work and performance, which in turn makes children feel less competent and confident, so that they need even more oversight."

Pamela Druckerman, a former reporter for the *Wall Street Journal*, moved to Paris after losing her job. She married a British expatriate and not long after that gave birth to a daughter. Less out of conviction than inexperience, Druckerman began raising her daughter, nicknamed Bean, *à l'Américaine*. The result, as she recounts in *Bringing Up Bébé* (Penguin Press), was that Bean was invariably the most ill-behaved child in every Paris restaurant and park she visited. French children could sit calmly through a three-course meal; Bean was throwing food by the time the apéritifs arrived.

Druckerman talked to a lot of French mothers, all of them svelte and most apparently well rested. She learned that the French believe ignoring children is good for them. "French parents don't worry that they're going to damage their kids by frustrating them," she writes. "To the contrary, they think their kids will be damaged if they can't cope with frustration." One mother, Martine, tells Druckerman that she always waited five minutes before picking up her infant daughter when she cried. While Druckerman and Martine are talking, in Martine's suburban home, the daughter, now three, is baking cupcakes by herself. Bean is roughly the same age, "but it wouldn't have occurred to me to let her do a complicated task like this all on her own," Druckerman observes. "I'd be supervising, and she'd be resisting my supervision."

Also key, Druckerman discovered, is just saying *non*. In contrast to American parents, French parents, when they say it, actually mean it. They "view learning to cope with 'no' as a crucial step in a child's evolution," Druckerman writes. "It forces them to understand that there are other people in the world, with needs as powerful as their own."

Not long ago, in the hope that our sons might become a little more Matsigenka, my husband and I gave them a new job: unloading the grocery bags from the car. One evening when I came home from the store, it was raining. Carrying two or three bags, the youngest, Aaron, who is thirteen, tried to jump over a puddle. There was a loud crash. After I'd retrieved what food could be salvaged from a Molotov cocktail of broken glass and mango juice, I decided that Aaron needed another, more vigorous lesson in responsibility. Now, in addition to unloading groceries, he would also have the task of taking out the garbage. On one of his first forays, he neglected to close the lid on the pail tightly enough, and it attracted a bear. The next morning, as I was gathering up the used tissues, ant-filled raisin boxes, and slimy Saran Wrap scattered across the yard, I decided that I didn't have time to let my kids help out around the house. (My husband informed me that I'd just been "kiddie-whipped.")

Ochs and Izquierdo noted, in their paper on the differences between the family lives of the Matsigenka and the Angelenos, how early the Matsigenka begin encouraging their children to be useful. Toddlers routinely heat their own food over an open fire, they observed, while "three-year-olds frequently practice cutting wood and grass with machetes and knives." Boys, when they are six or seven, start to accompany their fathers on fishing and hunting trips, and girls learn to help their mothers with the cooking. As a consequence, by the time they reach puberty Matsigenka kids have mastered most of the skills necessary for survival. Their competence encourages autonomy, which fosters further competence—a virtuous cycle that continues to adulthood.

The cycle in American households seems mostly to run in the opposite direction. So little is expected of kids that even adolescents may not know how to operate the many labor-saving devices their homes are filled with. Their incompetence begets exasperation, which results in still less being asked of them (which leaves them more time for video games). Referring to the Los Angeles families, Ochs and Izquierdo wrote, "Many parents remarked that it takes more effort to get children to collaborate than to do the tasks themselves."

One way to interpret these contrary cycles is to infer that Americans have a lower opinion of their kids' capacities. And, in a certain sense, this is probably true: how many parents in Park Slope or Brentwood would trust their three-year-olds to cut the grass with a machete? But in another sense, of course, it's ridiculous. Contemporary American parents—particularly the upscale sort that "unparenting" books are aimed at—tend to take a highly expansive view of their kids' abilities. Little Ben may not be able to tie his shoes, but that shouldn't preclude his going to Brown.

In "A Nation of Wimps: The High Cost of Invasive Parenting" (Broadway), Hara Estroff Marano argues that college rankings are ultimately to blame for what ails the American family. Her argument runs more or less as follows: High-powered parents worry that the economic opportunities for their children are shrinking. They see a degree from a top-tier school as one of the few ways to give their kids a jump on the competition. In order to secure this advantage, they will do pretty much anything, which means not just taking care of all the cooking and cleaning but also helping their children with math homework, hiring them S.A.T. tutors, and, if necessary, suing their high school. Marano, an editor-at-large at *Psychology Today*, tells about a high school in Washington State that required students to write an eight-page paper and present a ten-minute oral report before graduating. When one senior got a failing grade on his project, his parents hired a lawyer.

Today's parents are not just "helicopter parents," a former school principal complains to Marano. "They are a jet-powered turbo attack model." Other educators gripe about "snowplow parents," who try to clear every obstacle from their children's paths. The products of all this hovering, meanwhile, worry that they may not be able to manage college in the absence of household help. According to research conducted by sociologists at Boston College, today's incoming freshmen are less likely to be concerned about the rigors of higher education than "about how they will handle the logistics of everyday life."

One of the offshoots of the L.A. family study is a new book, *Life at Home in the Twenty-First Century* (Cotsen Institute of Archaeology), which its authors—the anthropologists Jeanne Arnold, of UCLA, Anthony Graesch, of Connecticut College, and Elinor Ochs—describe as a "visual ethnography of middle-class American households." Lavishly illustrated with photographs (by Enzo Ragazzini) of the families' houses and yards, the book offers an intimate glimpse into the crap-strewn core of American culture.

"After a few short years," the text notes, many families amass more objects "than their houses can hold." The result is garages given over to old furniture and unused sports equipment, home offices given over to boxes of stuff that haven't yet been stuck in the garage, and, in one particularly jam-packed house, a shower stall given over to storing dirty laundry.

Children, according to *Life at Home*, are disproportionate generators of clutter: "Each new child in a household leads to a 30 percent increase in a family's inventory of possessions during the preschool years alone." Many of the kids' rooms pictured are so crowded with clothes and toys, so many of which have been tossed on the floor, that there is no path to the bed. (One little girl's room contains, by the authors' count, two hundred and forty-eight dolls, including a hundred and sixty-five Beanie Babies.) The kids' possessions, not to mention their dioramas and their T-ball trophies, spill out into other rooms, giving the houses what the authors call "a very child-centered look."

When anthropologists study cultures like the Matsigenkas', they tend to see patterns. The Matsigenka prize hard work and self-sufficiency. Their daily rituals, their child-rearing practices, and even their folktales reinforce these values, which have an obvious utility for subsistence farmers. Matsigenka stories often feature characters undone by laziness; kids who still don't get the message are rubbed with an itch-inducing plant.

In contemporary American culture, the patterns are more elusive. What values do we convey by turning our homes into warehouses for dolls? By assigning our kids chores and then rewarding them when they screw up? By untying and then retying their shoes for them? It almost seems as if we're actively trying to raise a nation of "adultescents." And, perhaps without realizing it, we are.

As Melvin Konner, a psychiatrist and anthropologist at Emory University, points out in "The Evolution of Childhood" (Belknap), one of the defining characteristics of *Homo sapiens* is its "prolonged juvenile period." Compared with other apes, humans are "altricial," which is to say immature at birth. Chimpanzees, for instance, are born with brains half their adult size; the brains of human babies are only a third of their adult size. Chimps reach puberty shortly after they're weaned; humans take another decade or so. No one knows when exactly in the process of hominid evolution juvenile development began to slow down, but even *Homo ergaster*, who evolved some 1.8 million years ago, seems to have enjoyed—if that's the right word—a protracted childhood. It's often argued by anthropologists that the drawn-out timetable is what made humans human in the first place. It's the fact that we grow up slowly that makes acquiring language and building complicated social structures possible.

The same trend that appears in human prehistory shows up in history as well. The farther back you look, the faster kids grew up. In medieval Europe, children from seven on were initiated into adult work. Compulsory schooling, introduced in the nineteenth century, pushed back the age of maturity to sixteen or so. By the middle of the twentieth century, college graduation seemed, at least in this country, to be the new dividing line. Now, if Judd Apatow is to be trusted, it's possible to close in on forty without coming of age.

Evolutionarily speaking, this added delay makes a certain amount of sense. In an increasingly complex and unstable world, it may be adaptive to put off maturity as long as possible. According to this way of thinking, staying forever young means always being ready for the next big thing (whatever that might be).

Or adultesence might be just the opposite: not evidence of progress but another sign of a generalized regression. Letting things slide is always the easiest thing to do, in parenting no less than in banking, public education, and environmental protection. A lack of discipline is apparent these days in just about every aspect of American society. Why this should be is a much larger question, one to ponder as we take out the garbage and tie our kids' shoes.

1. Do you consider your upbringing "spoiled"? Why or why not? Did your view change after reading about Yanira at the beginning of the article?

2. What features of American culture might lead to a more spoiled upbringing?

WORKS CITED

Alibhai-Brown, Yasmin. "Hooray for Bollywood: 100 Years of Indian Cinema." *The Independent*. Independent Digital News and Media, 17 Mar. 2013. Web. 09 July 2013.

Carreiro, Heather. "Matador Network." *Matador Network*. Matador Network, 30 Apr. 2010. Web. 09 July 2013.

Fisher, Max. "Welcome to America, Please Be On Time." *The Atlantic*. The Atlantic, 1 June 2012. Web. 09 July 2013.

Flanagan, Jane. "Drunk Baboons Plague Cape Town's Exclusive Suburbs." *The Telegraph*. The Telegraph, 29 Aug. 2010. Web. 9 July 2013.

Hochschild, Arlie R. "The Nanny Chain." *The American Prospect*. The American Prospect, 3 Jan. 2000. Web. 09 July 2013.

Keaten, Jamey. "The Big Story." *Associated Press*. Associated Press, 1 Apr. 2013. Web. 09 July 2013.

Kelly, Jon. "Why British Police Don't Have Guns." *BBC News*. BBC, 19 Sept. 2012. Web. 09 July 2013.

Kolbert, Elizabeth. "Spoiled Rotten." *The New Yorker*. The New Yorker, 2 July 2012. Web. 09 July 2013.

Lin, Judy. "Honor or Abandon: Societies' Treatment of Elderly Intrigues Scholar." *UCLA Today*. University of California Los Angeles, 7 Jan. 2010. Web. 09 July 2013.

"Man Already Knows Everything He Needs To Know About Muslims | The Onion - America's Finest News Source." *Man Already Knows Everything He Needs To Know About Muslims. The Onion - America's Finest News Source*. The Onion, 30 Aug. 2010. Web. 09 July 2013.

Menzel, Peter, and Faith D'Aluisio. "Introduction." *Hungry Planet: What the World Eats*. Berkeley, CA: Ten Speed, 2007. 11-18. Print.

Miner, Horace. "Body Rituals Among the Nacirema." *Body Rituals Among the Nacirema*. N.p.: Irvington Publications, n.d. 50. Print.

Nafisi, Azar. "Chapter 1." *Reading Lolita in Tehran: A Memoir in Books*. New York: Random House Trade Paperbacks, 2008. 3-6. Print.

Partanen, Anu. "What Americans Keep Ignoring About Finland's School Success." *The Atlantic*. The Atlantic, 29 Dec. 2011. Web. 09 July 2013.

Rogers, Thomas. "For Help in Old Age, How about a New Age of Robots?" *HeraldTribune.com*. Herald Tribune, 17 Aug. 2012. Web. 09 July 2013.

Slaten, Kevin, and Xue Chao. "Wages Rising in Chinese Factories? Only for Some." *Wages Rising in Chinese Factories? Only For Some* -. In These Times, 18 Mar. 2013. Web. 09 July 2013.

Symmes, Patrick. "Thirty Days as a Cuban." *Harpers Magazine*. Harpers Magazine, Oct. 2010. Web. 09 July 2013.

Trethewey, Natasha. "On Whitman, Civil War Memory, and My South." *VQR On Whitman, Civil War Memory, and My South*. Virginia Quarterly Review, n.d. Web. 09 July 2013.

PERSPECTIVE